95

The
Family
Heart

The Family Heart

A Memoir of When Our Son Came Out

Robb

Forman

Dew

Addison-Wesley Publishing Company
Reading, Massachusetts . Menlo Park, California . New York
Don Mills, Ontario . Wokingham, England . Amsterdam . Bonn
Sydney . Singapore . Tokyo . Madrid . San Juan
Paris . Seoul . Milan . Mexico City . Taipei

"Halfway Down", from *When We Were Very Young* by A. A. Milne, Illustrations by E. H. Shepard. Copyright © 1924 by E. P. Dutton, renewed 1952 by A. A. Milne. Used by permission of Dutton Children's Books, a division of Penguin USA Inc.

"The Reflex" words and music by Duran Duran © 1983, reproduced by permission of Gloucester Place Music Ltd., London WC2H 0EA

Many of the designations used by manufacturers and sellers to distinguish their products are claimed as trademarks. Where those designations appear in this book and Addison-Wesley was aware of a trademark claim, the designations have been printed in initial capital letters (i.e., Rolodex).

Library of Congress Cataloging-in-Publication Data

Dew, Robb Forman.
    The family heart : a memoir of when our son came out / Robb Forman Dew.
        p.   cm.
    ISBN 0-201-62450-8
    1. Gay men—United States—Family relationships.   2. Parents of gays—United States.   3. Coming out (Sexual orientation)—United States.   I. Title.
    HQ76.2.U5D49   1994
    306.874—dc20   94-4010
                                                                        CIP

Jacket design by Jean Seal
Jacket painting by Gretchen Dow Simpson
Text design by Barbara Cohen Aronica
Set in 11-point Bembo by DEKR Corporation, Woburn, MA

1 2 3 4 5 6 7 8 9-ARM-9897969594
First printing, April 1994

For Charles and John

Contents

The
Family
Heart

Chapter One

Safe
as
Houses

FOR YEARS I ENVISIONED the passage of
time as a sort of steady trudge, not necessarily dreary, just relentless. It seemed to me that the
slipping by of the hours was an intangible certainty within
which one must accommodate all the events of a lifetime.
But it isn't so. For one thing, time accumulates from the
first moments of sensibility. The minutes accrue imper-
ceptibly into a stretch of history, and you turn around to
recognize, with amazement, your own past.

But also, some days have long legs. Now and then
an ordinary bit of time takes a yawning scissors step,
leaving you to scuttle along behind, scrabbling to cling to
ongoing events. I learned this late; when my children
were nearly full grown, because it was exactly such an

ordinary moment that enlarged and enlarged upon itself almost three years ago when my son told me he was gay.

It was early spring in New England, a soft day in May, and Stephen was home from his sophomore year at Yale until the first week of June, when he, my husband, Charles, and I would drive to Virginia to see his brother, Jack, graduate from Woodberry Forest School. When the phone rang, Stephen came around the corner from the TV room to answer it, and he stood at the far end of the kitchen, lounging against the long glass door to chat with Chloe. He was talking, and pausing to listen, and also keeping part of his attention on the CBS Evening News in the next room.

Earlier that day we had taken the paned-glass storm windows down and put up the screens on the two porches enclosing the kitchen. When I had come downstairs from my study to start dinner, I opened the kitchen windows for the first time that season and settled at the table to work the Jumble from the morning paper while occasionally tending the chicken I was roasting for dinner.

The kitchen is the only room in our house that doesn't have a direct view of the wide yard; the kitchen windows look out on the porches and then the lawn beyond, and the room is only dimly lit by natural light. But I like it just the way it is. It's fitted out with plain white cabinets and a white tiled floor, and, when we moved in, the walls were painted a searingly bright yellow. The effect, however, had been strangely and depressingly pallid, so we painted over the yellow with dark red—the color of New England barns—which did further darken the room but also freed it from its hopeless pretense of being bathed in sunlight. Our kitchen is a good place to cook or to think, to pay bills, to organize a checkbook. It's just an honest kitchen, a retreat at the center of the building, and it is where all our family's important information has been exchanged.

I was only passing the time, that afternoon, though, browsing through the paper and working the crossword puzzle and finally the Jumble. YEPCHS had stumped me. The words in the Jumble are either apparent immediately, or they are stubborn and require a little caginess to decipher. Three of the four words had been clear at first glance: BLAIS (basil), KRAPA (parka), and URADAM (maraud), but I was idly cheating by penciling variations of the fourth word and having no luck. The next morning when I picked up the paper to add it to the pile to be recycled, the Jumble caught my eye, and I immediately saw that the word was "psyche"—easier than all the others to figure out. But then, any puzzle seems to have been easy once you recognize it.

I'm not sure why I was suddenly alert to Stephen's end of the phone conversation. My attention was caught, I think, by some tone in his voice, or simply by the realization that his phone calls to or from Chloe were never particularly private; he never took the trouble to take the calls out of earshot of anyone else in the house. Chloe is a beautiful girl, sensuous and angelic looking at the same time, and she is funny and bright and endearing as well.

It might be that my ear was caught by what I didn't hear: there was no sense of the kind of tension that is inevitably there between two people as attractive and sexual as Chloe and Stephen. And by "sexual" I only mean the kind of magnetism that emanates from some people, especially older adolescents. Chloe and Stephen both possessed it, and, although I couldn't hear Chloe, Stephen's voice was nothing more than friendly. He was completely at ease; there was a certain edginess missing.

For a long time Chloe has been in our lives. We have even acquired a scattering of "Chloe" stories that are now and then retold at gatherings of mutual friends, just as we have acquired stories of various other of our children's friends. The tales themselves aren't what is important about the retelling of them; it is the connectedness they demonstrate. These stories, for instance, about Stephen's friend Joe, who spilled a bottle of Aqua Velva in the chemistry lab in the sixth grade, or Jack's friend Casey, who managed to lock everyone out of the car in the middle of a ski trip—the stories are fondly told, but they aren't really the point. The repetition of them, though, almost takes on the weight of ritual, because by reminding each other, over the Thanksgiving turkey, that we share a common history, we cut through the awkwardness of coming together again after a separation. These anecdotes are a sort of shorthand, and the people who figure in them are part of our family legend.

Chloe had been at school with Stephen since they were fourteen, and, in fact, two years earlier Chloe's parents and various of her siblings had settled next to us on the temporary bleachers set up at St. Paul's School in Concord, New Hampshire, to watch Stephen and Chloe's class graduate. Whatever failings St. Paul's School may have, it is a beautiful place, and the pageantry of graduation is dazzling. The girls are all in white dresses with ribbons or flowers in their hair, and the boys are in blazers and ties. The graduating seniors sit together, on a green sward that gently slopes to a lake, surrounded by parents and friends and a scattering of students from other classes. It is a glorious sight in good weather.

Chloe was sitting near us, wearing a wide-brimmed white hat with ribbons trailing down her back, and she and Stephen were not far apart in being called forward to receive awards and then diplomas. They were beautiful to see, smiling, healthy, with the wind from the lake ruffling Chloe's long hair and lifting the brim of her hat so that she reached up to hold it to her head as she approached the podium. Stephen was not far behind her, his own hair brushed back by the breeze, and congratulatory calls from friends in the group of students making him grin with his startling smile.

Chloe's mother leaned over to me and said, "Oh, don't you wish this were just their *wedding?*" And I knew exactly what she meant: their lives seemed perfect and uncomplicated and filled with amazing possibilities in that gorgeous afternoon; perhaps they could go on that way forever. I believe I simply began at that moment to think of Chloe as the probable romantic interest in Stephen's life. There were always friends of Stephen's around, male and female, but, at a certain point, both our sons made it clear that they wouldn't answer questions about their social lives.

It was a painful transition in Charles' and my lives as parents—during the time our sons were between the ages of about ten and thirteen—when either one of them, who had confided in us without hesitation, without even being asked, began to bristle at any question even remotely personal. I think it was painful because it was only Charles and I who were aware of the sudden change. One day Jack or Stephen was regaling us with amusing anecdotes or tales of school-related injustices, and the very next day one of us might ask that same child something as seemingly unremarkable as what he would like for lunch and be regarded with suspicion. It took a little while before we realized that this was a reasonable reserve—they were healthily uninterested in us, for the most part, and unnerved and surprised by our ongoing interest in them. So, in lieu of any information about Stephen's personal life, I jumped to a conclusion. I made one of many assumptions that parents should learn not to make about their children.

Two years later, though, in the kitchen on that afternoon in May, I only remember suddenly being aware—and being surprised by—the odd lack of interest in Stephen's voice. He was amiable—he is almost always amiable—but he wasn't reluctant to get off the phone, and Chloe was calling Massachusetts from the West Coast during prime time.

He hung up and turned away, heading around the corner to watch the end of the news, but I stopped him. "Steve?" And he paused in the doorway and turned toward me, and I continued, "Have you been involved with anyone at all? I mean romantically? Since St. Paul's?" Off and on, he had mentioned various girls in passing, and at St. Paul's there was always an assortment of girls lagging against the car and chatting with him whenever I was parked in front of his dorm while he loaded our station wagon. Girls phoned him often at our house, and he was invited for weekends away from school at the houses of girls who lived in wonderful places. But I hadn't heard him talk about any particular girl since he had been at Yale, although many phoned him when he was home.

For an instant he was surprised, and then he frowned, and I thought he was going to walk away in anger. There was a peculiar feeling of urgency and expectation in the room that I can only recall now; I can't re-create the sensation. But it was as if both of us had an intention to which we hadn't put a name—as hard to decipher as those scrambled words in the Jumble—although our intentions were loose from us and afloat in the air.

"There's something I've been meaning to tell you," he said finally.

We both fell silent, and then he moved forward a few paces toward me and was backlit by the gauzy light filtering from the screened porch through the glass-paned door. I couldn't read his face because of the shadow, but I know my children in all their moods; I am fairly good at deciphering the nuances of their postures—vulnerable or defensive or joyous. I may well know their very scent. Probably I could find them if I were blindfolded in a room full of people. I remember when they were little boys, and I would suddenly catch sight of one of my sons precariously balanced on a chair, or racing up or down the stairs, and I would experience the sensation of a fall he didn't take. It was a similar sensation I felt watching Stephen standing in the kitchen with his thumbs looped in the waistband of his jeans, his shoulders canted toward me, his head dipped slightly forward in determination. At once I wanted to raise my hands and gesture for him to stop what he was going to say, and I also wanted to urge him on and hear whatever it was. In fact, I sat as still as a stone. I didn't move at all.

"Of course I've been involved with someone since St. Paul's," he said. He wasn't frowning any longer; in fact, he had a slight smile that I knew from years of being connected to him. It was a smile that sought to protect me and Charles from any worry or irritation on his behalf. It's easy for me to classify it now, but looking at him then, as he stood in the shadowy room, I only perceived danger.

His tone and phrasing rang down the ranks of all the days I could remember and landed me resoundingly in the distant past where I was sitting in my bedroom in Baton Rouge in the twilight of a long-ago Louisiana evening, as the chameleons darted through the vines climbing up my window screens. My mother leaned into my room around the door frame, her heavy hair swinging forward in a parenthesis around her face. "By the way," she said, "after dinner I want to have a talk with you. There's something we need to discuss."

What my mother *did* eventually say to me, or why these two events should link themselves in my mind, I can't tell you. In both instances, however, I instinctively and immediately knew that I would never be eager to hear anything someone else had been considering so carefully. So three years ago in May, my son and I regarded each other warily.

"I think I might be gay," Stephen said.

In the instant before he spoke I'm convinced I knew what he was going to say, but at the same time I was uncertain that I understood. "Ah . . . well . . . you *think* you're gay?"

He looked perplexed, and anxious, too. "No, that's not what I mean. I mean I *am* gay."

This is such a difficult moment to remember, because the two of us had suddenly moved straight ahead into uncharted territory. I got up from the table and hugged him, and he held on to me, too, in a fierce embrace, lowering his chin to the top of my head. I felt light-headed, and my stomach clenched with dread. I had no idea what to do. "It doesn't make any difference to us," I said. "We love you no matter what."

We moved away from each other, both of us strangely embarrassed and without any rules of etiquette to cover this situation. Stephen seemed lost in his own house; he stood in the kitchen with a tentative air that more than anything in that elongated moment filled me with sorrow. His expression was precisely the curious gaze of assessment he had cast my way thirty minutes after he was born. He looked as though he wasn't at all sure that he could trust me.

Because I'm always on the lookout for misdirected impulsiveness—spontaneity that gets out of hand, that gets me into trouble—I rarely say anything entirely off the cuff. It's almost as if I *see* the words before they come out of my mouth, but I was baffled by what came out of my mouth next in my desperation to alleviate the uneasiness between me and this person I had loved for all his life. "Well, damn it, Stephen! I wish you'd told me years ago so I wouldn't have been stuck decorating the Christmas tree all by myself every year!" Since my children became teenagers, this has been my recurrent after-Christmas lament—tedious, now, to everyone who knows me, because I'm the only one who cares much if, or how, the Christmas tree is decorated at all.

He was as surprised as I by this peculiar outburst, and he merely looked at me blankly, and then he laughed. "Yeah. But I didn't think you'd want it decorated all in mauve." And then we both laughed; we were back on sure footing. We had humor between us again, but only fleetingly, because I had brushed off our discomfort with a sophistication and an attempted jauntiness I didn't yet possess, and I have no idea where such glibness came from.

This was one of those events in my life that, as I conjure it up in retrospect, appears to me like a pointillist painting, coming into focus hazily, at first, and slowly gathering the form of a whole experience. "Do you want to tell Dad and Jack?"

"I think it would be better if you told Dad. Do you mind doing that?"

"You know he won't care, Steve. He loves you."

"I know. But I just think it would be easier."

I don't know if he meant easier on him or easier on his father, and I suspect that it was a little bit of both, but mostly I think he yearned to avoid open embarrassment between the two of them.

"I don't think I should tell Jack yet," he said.

"Well, Stephen . . . " But he moved back into the other room and sat down in front of the television, although I thought he was as astounded as I was by the revelation of so much truth in the space of, perhaps, five or ten minutes. An atmosphere of unrelenting honesty is not hospitable, really, to domestic life. It is exhausting, since it bars the possibility of tactfulness or diplomacy.

Charles had dashed home from a history department meeting and gone upstairs to shower and change clothes before heading back to meet a prospective faculty member and introduce her to several other members of the department who would join them for drinks. He had been harried all semester, reluctantly chairing the department and teaching two courses. It seemed imperative that I tell him before he came face to face with Stephen, who would assume his father knew, but Charles was obviously in a hurry. He had scarcely noticed that I was standing next to him while he put on his tie in front of the vanity mirror. I put my hand on his arm to draw his attention, and then without taking the time to consider what I was doing, I simply said what I was determined to tell him.

"Listen, Stephen just told me he's gay, and he wanted me to tell you. I know it won't—"

"What? What did you say?" His words fell on top of my own, although he spoke slowly and softly, and he stopped still in the middle of adjusting his tie.

"Steve is gay. He wants you to know, but . . . "

He was moving away from me and out of the room as I spoke, and I followed him downstairs. Charles reacted exactly as I had to Stephen's news. In fact, he used almost the same words. "We love you, Steve. Nothing could ever change that." And he hugged Stephen and held onto him for a long moment. Both of us had the feeling that somehow Stephen was slipping away from us, as though he were being swept off by a strong current, and we wanted desperately to catch hold of him and pull him back to shore.

IT WOULDN'T BE FAIR TO SAY that I'm "house proud," but I suppose it's accurate enough to say I'm house besotted. When I was a little girl visiting my grandparents at Kenyon College, my grandfather would unfailingly disagree with me if I said that I loved ice cream, or my wonderful broomstick horsey that my mother had made for me, using a sock for its head, or my grandfather's own roses, which he tended with such passion.

"No, Robb," he would remonstrate gently and with great and hopeful patience, "you *like* your horsey. You *love* your mother. You *love* your father and your sister and your grandmother. You can't love your horsey, but you can like it very much."

"No, Pappy! I love him! I love him!"

He was a poet, and I know that words mattered a great deal to him. The trivialization of the word "love" would be hard for him to accommodate. I feel the same way whenever people offer to "share" something with me when they only mean they are going to *tell* me something.

My grandfather was right about the roses; he was right about the ice cream, but he was dead wrong about my stick horse. I loved it. And in the same way, I really do love my house. It has such a reassuring face, such comforting regulation and balance in its design. A child might draw it in crayon in the first grade as a generic house: a door in the center, two stories, two chimneys,

four windows facing forward on either side, and one
centered on the second story above the front door. When
I first saw it, the phrase "safe as houses" popped into my
head—a phrase I'd picked up through years of reading
British fiction, but that I'd never quite understood. I knew
immediately upon seeing it, however, that a family shel-
tering within such a sturdy structure should, by rights, be
immune from any terrible disharmony. It was safe as the
Bank of England, safe as the Rock of Gibraltar, safe as
houses.

We bought it from an estate even though the basement was flooded with over four feet of water, and all the
windows were nailed and caulked shut to keep out the
cold. It's almost two hundred years old, and when we
bought it, in 1978, it had last been renovated in 1946—
the year I was born. We have been working on it bit by
bit since we moved in, and the building does not seem to
me to be an inanimate object.

We live in a town of eight thousand people in the
farthest upper left-hand corner of Massachusetts. When
we first moved here from the South, I felt as though I had
arrived in a foreign country. The first time I entered the
small general store to get Bulldog hangers so we could at
last finish hanging our pictures, I was so unnerved by the
utter silence of the clerks who were standing about *not*
greeting me, that I slunk out the door without buying
anything and sat in my car, wondering what about me was
so offensive that no pretense of cordiality was made even
to ensure my business. I retreated that first day, but I
gradually began to understand the nonpresumptive quality
of New England courtesy. I've never been unhappy be-

cause of where I was living, but it is true that I've been happier in Williamstown than any other place I've ever lived.

Our house is sometimes very large and other times overcrowded. Locally, people often refer to it as big, sometimes as huge, but a friend of mine from Charleston, who lives in an antebellum mansion, summed it up as "cozy." During several weeks that May following Stephen's sophomore year at college, however, it was enormous. And the rooms of my house seemed to me, each one, a foreign country. The three of us ranged around that newly strange place in a paralysis of politeness, afraid that we would blunder into some area of hurtfulness of the other two.

I know now that Charles and I—even in our manner of acceptance—were unwittingly cruel, but either Stephen was so shocked by his act of revelation that he didn't notice, or he took us at our intention. We were doing the best we could with information that filled us with fear and sorrow and confusion.

My husband and I were well brought up; we are excellent products of middle-class Anglo-American be-havior. We kept our sorrow to ourselves. I found myself, at one point, standing under the hot water from the shower, cradling my head against the tiled wall and weep-ing and weeping, struggling with a thought that wouldn't come clear. "It would be easier if he were . . . " I had no idea how I meant to finish that sentence, nor did I know in what direction it was leading, until finally it occurred to me that I thought it would be easier for Stephen to have discovered he was black than to have realized that he was gay. When I had to admit to myself that I had had that thought—an idea so fraught with my own conveniently repressed knowledge of the hatred and inequity still extant in this country—I stood all alone under the running water and covered my face with my hands in embarrassment.

Stephen must not have known what to do next. Charles and I were relentlessly chipper and incurious over the few days following the day he told us he was gay. We didn't ask any questions at all, apparently less interested than if he had told us he had read a good book, and I don't remember that Charles and I even discussed these new circumstances with each other.

In the evenings we sat with books before us, but we didn't read; it requires reflection. We watched any sports we could find on television. There was no refuge in anything else on TV, because we discovered right away that, in 1991, the most innocent of sitcoms almost invariably had a passive but definite anti-gay agenda. Trotting out a stereotypical gay man—although rarely ever a lesbian—was apparently always good for a laugh. Or at least it filled a little time in those generally mindless scripts. How had we not noticed and been offended by it before? We watched a lot of baseball.

The second night I had a dream of dreaming. Even in my sleep I had to sneak up on myself, I think, because I love my children very much, and I couldn't bear to think that I had put either one of them in harm's way. I dreamed that I was asleep and having a dream in which I got out of bed and went into Stephen's room where he, too, was sound asleep and only eight or nine years old.

My dream of my dream-self began to speak to him. "I forgot to tell you something," the me of my dream's dream said, while my immediate dream-self looked on disapprovingly. "I think I forgot to tell you about sex." But Stephen didn't wake up; it was clear in the dream that he didn't need to know what I was saying, and the dream's me wandered slowly back to my own bed and—in the manner of an animated cartoon—merged with the me who I was dreaming was lying there next to my husband. I remember the feeling in the dream of absolute peacefulness.

The next morning, however, I awoke to a solid wall of speculation. Had I done this to my son? Had I tempted fate? After nearly seven years of struggling, I had just finished the manuscript of a novel, *Fortunate Lives,* which had been a difficult book to work on while my children were young, because in part it is about the death of a child. I had had to wait until my children were past the age of the child in the novel before I could conclude it. At last, though, I had completed it, and I was in that early stage of being done in which I was still in love with what I had created. Now it seemed to me that my euphoria about my own work had endangered my son, although the idea of what that danger might be was still amorphous; I hadn't named it yet.

Really, mothers have a hard time. We are so frightened for the welfare of our children that we believe we can barter with God—or fate—for their happiness. A divorced friend of mine has two small children who fly from Massachusetts to Seattle every summer to visit their father, and three weeks later they fly back again. While her children's plane is airborne, she scrubs the toilets and the bathroom floors, removes wax from the linoleum in her kitchen with boiling water, and scours her garbage cans with bleach in order to be sure she experiences not one bit of pleasure that God might tote up against the continued presence of her children on the earth. My friend knows this is nonsense; she *knows* she can't keep a plane from crashing by washing every window in her house, but she doesn't believe it. Or I may have that wrong; it may be that on some visceral level she is aware that she has no control over the safe transit of airplanes, but she may also know that if she were enjoying herself even slightly when something happened to her children, she would not only be emotionally devastated; she would feel punished.

I had managed to repress my acknowledgment that Stephen was somehow now imperiled until that peculiar dream the night before. And if Stephen was imperiled, then there must be some way in which it was my fault. The following morning I wandered around the house and looked out of the windows while trying to fend off an overwhelming sense of impending doom and an image of my own family's sudden isolation within our own town.

From the upstairs front hall window I gazed out at the street, at my neighbors' houses. Our road rises at a moderate incline to an ancient forest owned and protected by the college. The Williams College ski team roller-skis our hill; ambitious joggers pass by. At the top of the street, out of sight of our house, live the Michaelsons, an elegant couple, with children grown and gone. Bill Michaelson walks a brisk route past our property every day, walking stick in hand, tweed hat handsomely canted, his step purposeful. It was he who had stopped, though, to study the sign Jack and Stephen had nailed to our failing maple tree at the front gate when they were six and seven years old, respectively.

> *Dew Detective Agency*
> **Steve Dew. . . . Detective**
> **Jack Dew. . . . Associate**
> **(No case too small)**

My friend, Gail Godwin, was fond of my children and had sent them three splendid books on detecting, and Stephen and Jack were fascinated, reading all the detective stories they could find. Having read their way through mysteries written for children, such as the Encyclopedia Brown series, they had decided to try their own hand at sleuthing.

I saw Bill pause to read the sign with care, and I went to the door when he turned down our drive. As he approached I smiled in acknowledgment of what I knew was a sort of conspiracy, but he remained quite serious.

"I have a matter of importance to discuss with Detective Steve Dew and his associate, Jack Dew," he said. "I wonder if they're at home this afternoon?" Of course, he could see that they were at home, because they were sitting behind me at the kitchen table having lunch. I left the three of them alone, and Stephen and Jack eventually solved the "Case of the Barking Dog" for the Michaelsons.

And farther down the hill, on our other side, live the Hendriks. A large cannon resides on their front lawn, aimed, in fact, at the side of our house. I still have a copy of *The Slade Road Sentinel,* 1st Ed., Vol. 1, Steve Dew, Editor; Jack F. Dew, Editor. By the time they took up journalism, Jack was eight years old and far too canny to be persuaded by his nine-year-old brother to take second billing when the two of them decided to start a neighbor-hood newspaper. In their first and last edition, Stephen interviewed Mr. Hendriks for this story:

> The people of Slade Road might want to know the history of the cannon that sits on the Hendriks' lawn. The cannon was actually made from two wagon wheels, an axle, and a porch column all bought at an antique show in Greenfield. It is a replica of the Dahl Gren gun. The famous revolu-tionary Dahl Gren gun was used for naval and artillery purposes. Mr. Hendriks designed the replica, and he had to carve the porch column to resemble the barrel of the gun.

Charles decided out loud at dinner, after reading the article, that he would fashion a missile silo out of our barbecue grill and some leftover aluminum duct pipe in a Slade Road version of arms escalation. The boys were amused and simultaneously defensive of Mr. Hendriks's cannon, which is, indeed, impressive.

Almost a decade later, though, as I looked out at the street where we had lived for seventeen years, where my children had grown up, where we were when we heard the ongoing news of our far-flung families, and where we resided while incorporating into our perspective the evolution of world events, I was not feeling the loss of a sort of saccharine, Norman Rockwell existence. For one thing, that's never what we had on Slade Road or in the larger community of Williamstown. Life is always more complicated than that. I was contemplating the possible loss of approval, of communal acceptance on behalf of my son and the rest of us, too. I saw that we might plummet like stones if we were cast out of the familiar embrace of the community we were so accustomed to.

In setting up the detective agency, or putting together their newspaper, my sons were entering into a benign and unspoken contract with a few people to explore the mysterious customs and perimeters of adult behavior. Neither Stephen nor Jack *really* believed, even for a moment, that Bill Michaelson needed to find out why his dog barked unexpectedly during the day. Nor did they imagine that the residents of Slade Road wanted—only for the sake of new information—an edition of an amateur newspaper. I don't deny that they enjoyed behaving as if they were on an equal footing with the grown-ups whose collusion they needed to carry out these enterprises, but all the while they were having fun, they also knew it was a game. They were testing the waters of society, sounding the depths for goodwill, and they were extremely lucky to live in the midst of so much of it.

Standing alone in my front hall that spring so many years beyond my children's childhood, and trying to decipher the future, I don't think that I have ever felt more desolate. I looked out the window and knew that all the people Stephen had counted on for approval—all, of course, but his parents—might now regard him as a threat, an aberration, a stranger, rather than as a much-liked friend, a trusted neighbor, even something of a star in our small sphere. I found that the thought of any disapprobation, any lessening of regard for my own son, filled me with despair and some small, early flicker of ill-defined rage.

I considered the probable or possible loss of welcome in all the communities where our whole family had always been so much at home: Williamstown, itself; and Woodberry Forest School, which my husband had attended in the 1950s, and where he now served on the Board of Trustees, and from which my younger son would soon graduate; and Stephen's old school, St. Paul's, where he had seemed happy, and where I knew he had been valued.

I couldn't wrestle my new idea of my family into a shape I thought would be acceptable in the confines of any of these places. If our son were not damaged by the nature of his own sexual orientation, if we were not flawed by virtue of having a son who was gay, then why hadn't I ever heard mention of any other gay child or family of a gay child? If there was no context in any one of these communities for homosexuality then it must, indeed, be a terrible and shameful thing. And yet, I knew that there was nothing—nothing—terrible or shameful about Stephen.

I wandered up and down the stairs, in and out of the rooms, trying to reconcile all the disparate parts of our new situation. Finally I made coffee and sat down in the kitchen. I had only managed to conclude one thing; I had decided we should move to San Francisco. So unwittingly caught up in stereotypes was I, that our options seemed remarkably narrow.

Most of what I had read about homosexuality—and I hadn't read much, but since I read all the time I found that I had come across more than I realized—was in contemporary literature that had generally dealt with homosexuality as a tragic consequence of having a suffocating mother and a weak, indifferent, or absent father. I considered this for about twenty minutes. Had I been a suffocating mother? I don't know; I had meant to be a good mother, the best parent in the world. I had thought our family was a happy family, whatever that actually is. If I had smothered Stephen, then I had equally smothered my younger son, because, for better or worse, I love them equally. Was Charles weak, indifferent, or absent? Charles is probably the kindest man I've ever known, and he is certainly not indifferent to his sons, whom he loves deeply, nor has he been absent from their lives—literally or figuratively. My attempt at revisionist family history was only agonizing; it was getting me nowhere, and my fear for my son didn't bear investigation. So I put my reflections on hold and got up and went about my day in a state of limbo.

Charles and I pretended to an ease with the new status quo that we didn't feel. We had each quickly and independently fashioned a sort of ludicrous etiquette of feigned heartiness, because we couldn't have stood to have Stephen know he had thrown us into a state of grief. His revelation had shattered our expectations of who he was.

We pretended that his sudden emergence as a gay man in what we had considered our conventional family was a matter of no consequence, something that had slipped from our minds completely.

In the South of the '50s and '60s, where Charles and I grew up, we had each separately concluded—unwittingly, and simply by observation—that it was difficult, maybe tragic, to be black. In my own family no one ever said this; my parents were pro-integration, and I doubt that they thought blacks were unequal to them in any way. Nevertheless, the message was everywhere around us in the legally imposed separation of the races, in the fact of whites-only swimming pools, water fountains, and restaurants. Therefore, and without public or private discussion, those white people who considered themselves enlightened or progressive assumed that it would be the height of unkindness and tactlessness to acknowledge that someone else was black.

The only transgression of this unspoken taboo that I can remember occurred on the Monday after the 1963 bombing of the Sixteenth Street Baptist Church, a Black church in Birmingham, Alabama, and the resulting deaths of four little girls who had been attending Sunday school.

My mother met our housekeeper, Lizzie Rogers, a black woman, at the door when she arrived for work the next morning, and my father was just behind them. "Oh, Lizzie," my mother said, "sometimes I'm so ashamed to be white!"

I don't know what else they said to each other just then, but I do remember my father later, sounding baffled and offended, arguing with my mother. "How could you say that, Helen? That was a terrible thing to say." He didn't want to be part of a collective guilt, and I always thought he believed my mother had somehow hurt Lizzie's feelings. But he was absolutely wrong in his disapproval of my mother's having said anything, or in his disapproval of what she said. I wish I had remembered that myself in 1991.

The three of us spent several days occupying the rooms in a state of careful good cheer. Charles and I were busy all the time; we never settled very long in one place, and I don't know what Stephen must have thought, but eventually he approached us in the late afternoon where we were sitting on the screened porch in the balmy air.

"Steve!" Charles said, "would you like some iced tea? Or a beer?" His voice was warm, perhaps overly exuberant.

"Yeah. Thanks. I'll get some iced tea. Do you want anything?"

"I'd love some tea, Stephen, if it's not too much trouble," I said, beaming at him. I was so nervous that my mouth went dry. Stephen has my father's family's brown eyes—an orange brown, the iris rimmed with black—and arched brows, and his expression caught my attention that afternoon because it was filled with compassion. I think now that it struck me so forcefully because he was only nineteen years old, but his expression held far more empathy than anyone that age usually possesses.

He brought our glasses of tea from the kitchen and sat down, too, not saying anything for a few moments, and then he looked directly at us, still with an expression of gentle tactfulness. He gazed at Charles and me steadily while he spoke, probably afraid we would find some chore to take us off if he didn't say what he wanted us to hear. "Listen, I know this must be really hard for you. I just want you to know how much it means to me to know that it doesn't change the way you feel about me."

"Nothing could ever change the way we feel about you, Steve," Charles said. "We love you more than you know."

"We do, sweetie," I said.

"I *do* know. But it must be hard for you," he said, "because I know you didn't expect this. I just wanted to tell you that you can ask me anything you want to know. I mean, you must wonder about a lot of things. I don't want to have any secrets. . . . I don't want you to feel uncomfortable around me." This was a terrible admission—a plea—from my own son, and I tried not to let myself start crying. "I'll be glad to answer any questions you want to ask," he said.

All around the porch the lilac bushes were in bud, with just a few blooms among the branches, so that their delicate scent reached us only when a breeze picked up, but I remember the smell of lilacs in conjunction with Stephen's words, and the combination was such a generous offering in the mild weather that it was very nearly heartbreaking.

Chapter Two

Familiar Weather

A LMOST TWENTY YEARS AGO on an early spring day in Missouri, I was outside with the children, wrestling Jack into his infant carrier in the front seat of the car while Stephen waited to climb into the back. Suddenly the three of us startled—the way I've seen deer freeze in place when they are grazing in the meadow behind our house and our dogs begin to bark. I stopped still in the midst of settling Jack comfortably in his padded carrier. Stephen went rigid against the car, and even Jack, not yet two years old, was round-eyed and quiet with attention. I remember quite clearly the feeling I had of unspecified alarm.

Until that moment I had never taken into account the continual movement of the air, the gentle drifts, small eddies and fluid currents of motion generally so subtle that they aren't noted. But all at once to be inhabiting a space in which the air goes still, as it did momentarily that afternoon, is a jolt to the nervous system. The hair on my arms prickled, and the light filtering through the row of soft maples that bordered our lawn had an odd quality of apparent weight, as though it had taken on mass, and it was shot through with an edgy yellow-green.

It seemed that every natural motion had come to a halt, and then a great turbulence of sand and loose gravel rose from the area of a dredging operation a mile or so away on the banks of the Missouri River. I remember looking on at the whirling debris with puzzlement, not realizing that utter quiet had fallen until the next moment when we were astounded by noise—not like the rumble of an oncoming train, but the grainy friction of a million tiny things, like the grinding of the earth's teeth. Beneath that overriding uproar were other small explosions of sound—the relatively quiet hiss and jangle of glass breaking and whirling into the air, which later proved to have been all the windows of our house exploding outward.

After a moment the great rush of noise became particular: I could hear the separate sounds of the wind blowing, branches splintering, the slap of leaves, Jack's astonished shriek, and Charles calling from inside the house, all of which were comfortingly familiar after those few moments of existing within a phenomenon of huge sound without apparent origin. The air rushed everywhere at once, and I left the car door hanging open against the force of the wind. The children and I got into the house, and the wind buffeted the building, rattling the shard-studded frames of the shattered windows, billowing the curtains, and blowing rain and leaves into the rooms. And then it was gone, as if that rushing air had been corporeal, racing along the river and leaving disarray everywhere in its wake. All at once the rain no longer surged but fell reasonably to earth in a spring shower.

Outside, along the two main streets of Rocheport—a village of three hundred people—parts of roofs were gone, peeled back in a curl if they were tin, and lifted right from the beams if they were asphalt shingles. Many flowering trees, or those in new leaf, were stripped bare while others remained untouched, and everywhere there was the gritty, glassy film of sand the wind had left behind.

I don't know what it was; officially this weather was not classified as a tornado. The farmers in town called it a wind burst, and that sounds right to me. It was a perfectly natural but unprecedented, unexpected, meteorological outburst, which was over in minutes, but which left us in its aftermath standing stunned within our house among leafy, drenched debris unreasonably strewn across the wood floors. Now that we could not escape the fact that we were subject to such turmoil, and now that our idea of shelter—of safety—was revealed to us as pregnable, we muddled about for some time in appalled disorientation, because we had lost our frame of reference.

And that was the state in which Charles and Stephen and I found ourselves seventeen years later as we sat on the porch in the soft spring of New England doing our best to figure out how to traverse the altered landscape. It saddens and enrages me, now, that when Stephen sat with us on the porch and offered to tell us anything we wanted to know, we were fairly feeble in our attempts to take him up on it, because we didn't even know enough to be clear about what we needed to find out.

Stephen tried to take over, filling in for us and making conversation as best he could.

"I know this is hard for you," he said again, and his father and I only looked back at him; we didn't know what would be all right to ask. We sat on the porch looking out at the side yard where the dogs lay on the crest of our hill so they could monitor the goings-on of the street. They are two German shepherds, impressive only from a distance, but they lay where the slight breeze ruffled their coats, their heads raised to catch the scent of whatever was in the air, settled back to back, like bookends. They looked fairly regal arrayed against the new spring grass that is a poignantly sweet green, unlike any green I've seen in any other part of the world. Each year I am moved by the landscape of New England after the long winter. The fragile green that appears like mist in the tops of distant trees and, day by day, extends farther up the hills toward the mountaintops is exactly the color that optimism would be if it had color.

The dogs were in the yard; Jane Melrose was taking her corgi for his daily constitutional; a pair of joggers passed by, slowing on the hill and talking to each other, but we could only hear their voices; we couldn't discern their words. Everything was exactly as it always had been, and yet all three of us were disoriented and apprehensive. Our long-held and mutual idea of ourselves as we existed in relation to each other lay around us in disarray.

Stephen was striving mightily to put us at ease, and I believe Charles and I realized simultaneously that this desperate courtesy toward his own parents was something no child should have to employ.

"You know, Stephen," Charles said, "we don't know much about all this." His voice was careful, and he hesitated before saying more. "But I guess I'm most worried about whether or not you're okay. I'm worried about how you are. I mean about your health. If you don't mind if I ask you that?"

I was so afraid of what Stephen's response might be that I didn't turn to see his face. My sense of foreboding was enormous. I had the feeling of being caught up in something terrible that was in the process of happening to us. The three days that had passed since he told us he was gay had lapsed slowly, with little conversation. Time had become sluggish and slow to turn. Now that one of us had asked this question at last—even though Charles and I hadn't spoken this terror aloud to each other—I wanted to know the answer, whatever it was, and yet I didn't want to see in Stephen's expression any news I didn't think I could bear to hear.

"I hope you'll ask me anything you want to know. I really mean that." Stephen was insistent and soft-voiced. "But I'm okay. I'm fine. You mean AIDS? No, I'm okay."

Charles and I should have been giddy with relief, but we knew so little that we merely filed this away for the time being and didn't even rejoice appropriately.

I turned back from watching the neighborhood and glanced at Stephen, who looked so sad and tired beneath his careful expression of goodwill that my eyes filled with tears in spite of myself. I was embarrassed and chagrined; I've never thought of myself as a person who cries easily or publicly.

Stephen leaned toward me just slightly. "You don't have to be sad, Mom," he said.

But I didn't dare reply for fear of becoming teary, again; I only shook my head and waved away his concern. In that moment it was he who was the adult among us. He had said to me what I had meant to say to him.

Finally I framed a question that was more like a plea. "But, Steve, what about Jessica? You remember? In the seventh grade? Or Amy? You took Amy to her prom. And Chloe? So many girls at St. Paul's? Are you sure about this, sweetie?" I meant for my voice to be as gentle as possible; I didn't intend to be aggressively inquisitive, but an expression of despair crossed Stephen's face—almost a grimace. He looked away, but I pressed on. "What I mean is, is this something you're just going through? Just a stage? Is it something you've chosen? I mean . . . are you *angry* at us? Or maybe especially at me? Are you trying . . . I don't know . . . to *rebel* against the sort of life we live? Trying not just to be . . . oh . . . bourgeois, or something?" Aside from Stephen's revelation to us, Charles and I were in a peculiar stage in our lives as parents, with both our sons growing beyond our influence, but, even so, surely it was more than strange that neither of us was struck by the astounding solipsism, even the arrogance, of the idea that Stephen's sexuality—whatever it might be—revolved around us.

And Stephen took a long breath. "Ah, Mom . . . " His hands had been curled in fists on his knees as he sat rocked back in a straight-legged chair, but he opened his palms outward, letting the chair fall forward and once again leaning toward us. "God. Something I've *chosen!* I

The Family Heart • 33

don't think this is anything that *anyone* would choose in this society. I didn't plan this. You don't understand. Even at St. Paul's I used to take long walks by myself and think, 'I can't let this happen! I *won't* let this happen! I'm not going to feel this way!' I didn't wake up one day and think it would really be *interesting* to be gay."

"No, no. Well, of course not," I said. I believed his answer as much as I could, brought up as I was on watered-down Freud, but mostly, in that instant, I was appalled at this new idea of Stephen at St. Paul's School, feeling such anguish, being absolutely alone in a place where he excelled at almost everything he did and was loved by his friends and teachers. This new picture was a direct contradiction of the idea of him I had held in my head for so many years—an image of Stephen among the friends who were always surrounding him whenever I caught sight of him as I waited at his dorm, or stood chatting with his roommate's parents, who live in a faculty house on the St. Paul's campus. This new and bewildering idea of his isolation was dreadful to me, and, as with so much that Stephen offered to us on that temperate afternoon, so many questions he strove to answer honestly and with dignity, I only heard it obliquely. I see now that I didn't know how to incorporate anything he told us into my view of the real world. I didn't know how to listen to what he was saying without relating it to how it made *me* feel—or how I imagined it might make Charles feel. Had Stephen been much younger than age nineteen, my self-involvement would have bordered on irresponsibility. As it was it was merely unkind.

Charles and I had no attention to spare, just then, for

anyone but ourselves. We were suffering a temporary loss
of empathy and even of generosity. We were desperate to
discover how to restore our peace of mind. I offered
Stephen a lament. "But, Steve, what about children?
You'll never have children!" My voice broke, and for the
first time since he had come out to us, Stephen let his
guard down for a moment.

"God! Mom! Don't you see. . . . " His words were
explosive, and Charles and I were startled, but Stephen
paused for a moment and calmed his voice. "The thing
is," he said, "I just want what you've *got*. I think that's
what everybody wants even if they don't know it. Even
if they don't understand that's what they want. Because
how can I get anything else—any work I really care
about—how can I get anything important *done* if I don't
have some kind of . . . evenness? How can I be happy?"
This last seemed to be a real question; he looked at us
expectantly, but we gazed back at him perplexed, not
understanding that he may have hoped for an answer.

He slowed his speech and moderated his tone even
more, in an effort, I think, to allow us to catch up to him,
in an amazing leap of empathy for us. He was calm and
earnest and carefully instructive. "I'd like there to be a
person I love who loves me, but I don't know if that'll
ever happen. I've always wanted to have children. I'd be
a good father, and children ought to have good parents!
Jack and I do. But I can't tell if I'm even going to be able
to live a life that won't be *defined* just by the fact that I'm
gay. I just want to do the things I care about. I don't want
to have to think about being gay every minute of my life!
I wish that this could just be one of about ninety things

people would think about when they think about me. I wish it could just be nothing."

Charles and I were beyond replying for a little while, and I neglected even to take into account the sad precocity of a nineteen-year-old who has considered all this. Eventually I only nodded in agreement. "I've always thought you'd be a great father. Any child would be lucky to have either you or Jack as parents." I was surprised that my saying so appeared to make Stephen feel even worse, because I must have meant to be comforting.

At least in this I thought I understood Stephen's regret very well, because one of the first bits of grief that I had been able to identify immediately after he told me he was gay was the idea that there would never be a child of Stephen's in the world.

Without even being conscious of the many years over which I had constructed so many assumptions, I had invested a great deal in the idea that my children would know the passionate involvement of being a parent. I counted on their eventual parenthood whenever the fact of my own motherhood was the greatest satisfaction of my life, and, too, during those times when I knew I was failing at it. It sometimes seemed to me, in moments of absolute euphoria as my children were growing up, that they could not possibly understand how much they are loved by me unless they love some child of their own in the same way. But at other times, when I felt desperately inept and maternally clumsy, I thought that if either of my sons didn't have children, how would he ever be able to forgive my failures? And, also, there are no children I would rather know than the children of my own children.

That was what I was thinking. It didn't occur to me that my easy concurrence in his distress might not be what Stephen was hoping for.

In Louisiana, where I grew up, spring is astonishing in its exuberance, sating one's senses with the pungent, heavy scent of gardenias blooming abundantly in every yard and floated in crystal bowls on coffee tables and sideboards. But the smell of a New England spring is the loamy scent of the earth itself—more evocative of fecundity, really, than the perfume of springtime in Baton Rouge. In the Northeast, however, the evidence of new growth appears gradually, and inevitably suffers setbacks of late frosts and odd snow storms.

Generally in late February and early March, often with snow still on the ground, sap starts running in the maples, and taps are set and pails hung even from the trunks of town trees, which every spring surprises me once again—such an earthy endeavor carried out right there in the front yards of Main Street. And where the mountains have been gashed and blasted to make way for roads, the striated rocks rising on either side are draped with clumps of dripping icicles and are silvery with thin, winding rivulets of water as the snow melts on the mountaintops. The streams and rivers rise and gush with new accumulations, and in the basements sump pumps whir and thump with greater frequency as the earth thaws. Householders awaken in the night if the pump is too long silent. Spring in New England is not sentimental like the extravagant spring I knew in the South; it is a discreet and liquid season. So maybe my private weeping in that May was appropriate.

The spring of 1991 was the only time in our marriage when Charles and I employed courtesy to each other in lieu of conversation. I was inexperienced at the sorrow I accommodated; I was filled simultaneously with an inexplicable yearning—akin to homesickness—and the certainty that my sorrow was some sort of treachery toward my son. Knowledge and rationality didn't help much, and it seemed to me that this sadness that obsessed us that spring was more than Charles and I could sustain: humor slipped away, even ambition and hope and the idea of the possibility of joy deserted us, very much as if someone had died.

The memory of this indulgence of grief is shameful to me now, because, all the while I felt as if I were in mourning, Stephen was right there with us, alive and healthy and kind, filled with worry and compassion for his own parents.

In the mornings I tried to work at my writing, but it's a reflective business, and inevitably I fell into melancholy brooding. I could not shake the image of Stephen all alone, tracing the beautiful paths that crisscross the grounds of St. Paul's School, through the woods and around the ponds, climbing the hill behind the old library with his long, loping stride. It was a picture as vivid as if it were an actual memory, and I harbored and wept over it when I was alone. It was unbearable that he had ever been so isolated among people who held him in high regard, among all those glorious teenagers who astonished me with their collective physical beauty every time I was on campus.

I thought of a teacher at St. Paul's who had been in

the admissions department and interviewed Stephen when he was looking at independent schools. Two years later she had drawn me aside during parents' weekend and said, "You know, occasionally we've made some bad admissions decisions at St. Paul's, and generally we make good admissions decisions. We usually put together a pretty good class. But now and then we make a *brilliant* admissions decision. Steve was one of those. He was a brilliant decision! I'm so glad he decided to come here!"

Earlier that same morning I had overheard a tearful daughter protesting to her anxious parents, "Dad, we saw *eight* schools in four days! This is *not* the school I thought I was going to. I think I'm supposed to be at Groton."

Once Stephen had become determined to go away to school, the search and decision-making had been intense and grueling. After the misery of waiting to find out if he would be accepted at the schools to which he finally applied, he had decided on St. Paul's instead of Andover, Exeter, or St. Georges. On that warm Saturday of our second parents' weekend, milling about among baffled, worried parents, and seeing how Stephen had thrived, it seemed to me that he had made the perfect choice. Ms. Brewster and I grinned at each other in mutual pleasure and congratulations.

But now, two years after Stephen had graduated from St. Paul's—two years after that lovely afternoon at the lake where he was among so many people who admired him and regarded him with deep affection—I could not allow myself even to think about his spectacular school career. For some reason, it filled me with sorrow more than any other memory.

I was unusually homesick for Jack, even though it was he who was away and I who was at home. I don't know how else to describe what I felt: it was a longing for the comfort of familiarity. I wanted him with us, because I loved him, of course, but also because I felt that we were all somehow threatened, and I had a nearly obsessive desire to circle the wagons, to keep us together and to keep everyone else out.

As Jack's graduation present, Charles and I were giving Jack and Stephen a six-week course at a language institute in Oaxaca, Mexico, and, following that, four more weeks of travel through the rest of the country. Stephen had six years of Spanish and Jack three, but neither of them had ever had the chance to live among people for whom it is the native tongue. The two of them would be flying out of Dulles airport in Washington the afternoon following the morning graduation ceremonies at Woodberry Forest. The logistics of attending all the graduation events, packing up four years' worth of Jack's accumulated possessions, and getting the two of them to Washington on time required careful planning and a good deal of phoning back and forth to Jack.

Whenever I spoke with Jack, however, I felt as though we had become a counterfeit family. The three of us in Williamstown were engaged in an inescapable and kindly meant deceit of Jack while he finished the last of his four years at his school in Virginia, and it was hard on all of us. Our motives sprang from the desire not to hurt any one of us more than we already were distressed one way or another.

And, after all, Jack and Stephen have their own

history together—not entirely apart from us, of course, because how could it be? But their relationship is bound to be as complicated as that of any siblings, and it has its own dynamic, which Charles and I will never know entirely and which isn't really our business. It was Stephen's decision not to tell his brother, and he agonized over it when I demurred.

"I feel like we're *conspiring* against him in some way," I said. "Not telling him something the rest of us know. It doesn't seem right to me, Steve. I'm afraid it will hurt his feelings to find out we kept this a secret from him."

There are rare days in the Berkshires when a haze moves in from some distant, polluted, urban area, and the mountains that rise beyond the vista of our meadow are obscured. The effect is curious; during those few days it's as though our house is set down upon a flat cake plate over which someone has placed a cover. It's unpleasantly claustrophobic, and it always makes me restless, with the feeling that in just a moment the normal clarity of the atmosphere will return. I become unreasonably distracted and edgy.

I think Stephen felt the same way, particularly being enclosed with me on the screened porch when I was pressing him once again about telling Jack. He got up and moved to the end of the porch where he stood looking out at the barely discernible mass of the mountains rising in the distance.

"This isn't the right time. For one thing, it's his graduation. It should be about him. If I tell him now, the whole thing will be ruined for him. And for four years

he's been at an all-male, conservative southern school,"
he said.

"Well. Jack's *male,* but he's not conservative, and he's
not southern. And I don't think that would matter, anyway. Woodberry has some of the most moderate, open-
minded, decent faculty of any school I've ever seen.
Including St. Paul's."

Charles was serving a term on the board of trustees
at Woodberry Forest School, and I had come to admire
several people on the Woodberry faculty with whom
Charles often dealt, especially Jack's advisor, Daniel Elgin.
In fact, many of the phone calls from Jack had been about
his worry over choosing a gift for Mr. Elgin that would
adequately express his fondness for and appreciation of the
whole Elgin family. Eventually Jack found a shop in Orange, Virginia, that sold handsome wooden rocking
chairs, which he thought would be just the right gift, one
that could be used on the Elgins' recently constructed
back porch that looks out over the Blue Ridge Mountains. Jack wanted a small plaque with an inscription
mounted on the back of the chair, and I had volunteered
to take on that project, but that entailed even more
phoning back and forth to Virginia, so Jack's ignorance of
all that was going on at home was very much on my mind,
and I was relentless in urging Stephen to take Jack into
his confidence.

"I didn't even come *out* when I was at St. Paul's,
Mom. When I was Jack's age. And just think about it!
Oliver North's son goes to Woodberry Forest. There've
got to be boys at Woodberry who are gay, but they

wouldn't come out at that school. I'll tell Jack when it's the right time. I want him to know."

"Oh, sweetie, just tell him, then. If you really think this is the wrong time, then wait until after graduation. But it's not fair to keep him in the dark when all the rest of us know. I mean, Steve, even your good friends know, and they're friends of Jack's, too. It's just not right to have him find out from a friend. It would be like . . . well, it would be like . . . oh, hearing that your brother was a mass murderer, or something!"

My hands flew to my mouth too late to stop the words I had just said, and Stephen turned around, away from the haze-shrouded mountains. His voice was un-inflected, a low monotone. He looked as stunned as if I had struck him. "No," he said. "No, Mom. I hardly think it would be like finding out I was a mass murderer. Is that how you see it?"

I had started crying without sound, although I didn't realize it until I tried to speak and couldn't control my voice. "My God! Oh, God. No! Of course that's not how I see it." But that's what I had said; I had likened my own son to a deranged killer, when all I knew about Stephen now that I hadn't known before was that if he loved someone it would be a man. What had happened? Where had that thought come from, and why had I allowed myself to utter it? Stephen stayed away from me at the far end of the porch, his expression of open hopefulness gone entirely, his whole posture drawn in and closed away from me.

I was desperate to undo this damage. "What I'm trying to say is that it's the last thing he would ever imagine! It's a thing he will never have thought of. It would be as if . . . oh . . . as if he heard from, say, his friend Mark that Dad and I were getting a divorce. That's what I'm trying to say, Stephen. It would be unimaginable to him. I mean, Dad and I aren't ever going to get a divorce, because we wouldn't ever want to, and Jack knows that absolutely. So, you see . . . you see? That's what I was trying to say."

Stephen loosened a little and folded his arms across his chest, leaning back against the screen and squinting at me slightly for a long moment. "But, Mom, if that's the first comparison you thought of—if the first analogy that crossed your mind was that Jack would be as upset to find out I'm gay as he would be to find out I was a mass *murderer*—well, why do you want me to tell him?"

Stephen's tone was slightly guarded, but it wasn't hostile. In fact, it was a tone that tried to disguise from me the fact that I had hurt him.

"Oh, God! I'm so sorry. I'm so sorry. I don't know what's happening to me!" I really meant it. I had astounded myself with my own cruelty. Most parents love their children, and to continue to proclaim my devotion for my children strips the declaration of any potency. But, in my case, I really didn't understand, or even entirely believe, that unconditional love could exist until I felt it for my sons. It was only good luck that they turned out to be people who I care about so deeply beyond mere maternal instinct that the idea of my life without that sustaining warmth is unfathomable. It is horrible to remember that I caused a child of mine such pain, but Stephen's patience that summer was seemingly limitless.

"I only want to be sure that Jack hears this from one of us," I said. "Of course, you're right, though. It has to be up to you. But I was wondering if it would be easier if Dad or I told him? Whenever you think it's the right time?"

Stephen still stood at the far end of the porch, and he didn't reply for a moment, and when he did his voice was strained. "But suppose I lose him?" Stephen said. "What if he just can't deal with it? What will I do if I lose him?"

I didn't know what to say. I was at sea. "That won't happen, Stephen. I can't believe that will happen. And if it does happen—or if he has some trouble with it for a while—then it will be his problem." I said this, but it was an agonizing idea to consider for either of my sons, and Stephen was shocked.

"How can you say that to me? How can you even think that? Of *course* it won't be *his* problem!" His voice was loud and startling in the muted, hazy afternoon. "He's my *brother!* I love Jack. I don't know what it would be like if I lost him."

WHAT ON EARTH COULD TOLSTOY HAVE BEEN THINKING when he wrote the opening line of his masterpiece, *Anna Karenina*: "Happy families are all alike; every unhappy family is unhappy in its own way." It's a great line—hard not to use, I suppose, once he'd come up with it—but the untruth of it is breathtaking. Tolstoy didn't go in much for a clever line; he was pretty straightforward, at least in translation. Small ironies didn't seem to interest him, and I don't think he gave a moment's thought to the astonishing sweep of such an assertion. The idea of happiness as applied to something as complex as a family is wrongheaded anyway.

In fact, I grew up in a family made up of remarkable people who were not very happy collectively, and I would say that we were much like every other unhappy family. Unhappy families are various only by the degree of their misery. But my immediate family of my husband and two children has been as happy as any family can be, and we are not much at all like any other family that has managed to adhere with a degree of contentment—which I think is probably the most accurate definition of a "happy family."

But we were foundering that spring. Familial ease is a mysterious thing; it can't be engendered; it simply exists. It has to do with a combination of trust, mutual knowledge of one another's history, and unconditional affection. I don't know what had slipped away from us. I suppose we all felt as if, all of a sudden, we didn't know each other as well as we thought we did, and Stephen must have wondered if all that affection in which he was held would prove to be less than unconditional. It didn't occur to Charles or me that, even though we had assured him that we loved him, Stephen might not remain convinced that he was loved in the same way—utterly without reservation—as he knew he had been loved before he came out. We should have understood this better, but we were stupid with shock after having our assumptions pulled out from under us.

Stephen had not told us it was all right to make any of this information public knowledge, and Charles and I wouldn't have known how to go about doing that, anyway. As far as Charles and I knew, there was no other family who had ever known they had a gay child. There was no social construct to catch us as we flew apart. We felt overwhelmingly isolated in spite of the fact that two of my closest women friends had been a couple for several years, and two of Charles's favorite younger colleagues are openly gay and lesbian. I have no idea why none of this occurred to us as relevant. Perhaps it was because we only knew these people as successful adults; it didn't occur to us that they had once been children, had—each one—at some time been defined only as being someone's child. But I think that's too simplistic an explanation. I suspect our feeling of isolation had more to do with our mindless acceptance of the public view of homosexuality as being a subject that must not be discussed, that is taboo.

We were simply stunned with apprehension and sorrow, and we didn't know what to do about it. We didn't know where to seek relief. Charles was still teaching, but he began to avoid the history department's weekly lunch at the Faculty Club, especially since Williams College commencement was at hand, and his colleagues were apt to wax nostalgic about their children and to be interested in the welfare of their friends' children. Of course, if he were asked about Jack's and Stephen's progress, Charles could have offered simple, neutral answers, but even early on that felt wrong; it felt like betrayal. We have never been ashamed of Stephen, and silence or disingenuousness on his behalf seemed like a manifestation of shame.

I prowled the local grocery stores and the organic food store at off-hours. Inevitably, of course, I ran into people I knew, but I passed them by with ferociously cheerful greetings. "Elise! How are you? And how's Tom? He's wonderful, I'm sure!" I discovered that if you provide people with answers, they seldom try to offer you any other information, and they are stopped in the midst of any possible query about your own state of affairs. But now and then I was caught in conversation, and it made me miserable to be trapped among the canned tomatoes and asked anything about myself or my family.

"Robb, I haven't seen you in ages. I hope you're at work on a new book. I'm just waiting for another one. And how are your wonderful sons? It's so strange that our children are all growing up. Steve must be a sophomore by now. He and Jonathan are the same age, aren't they? I can't remember, it's been so long since they were at the public schools together. And how's Jack? He must be about to graduate from high school." This kindly interest was unbearable, because I had no idea what to say.

Those many years ago, in the aftermath of that violent windstorm in Missouri, I had set up webbed lawn chairs and chaises longues in our dank, earth-floored basement. Whenever tornado warnings were issued, Charles and I gathered blankets and candles and took the children down there to sleep. In the pleasant and unthreatening weather of the New England spring of 1991, I nevertheless longed to retreat once again to that basement in Missouri, taking my children with me and bundling them comfortably in the flimsy lawn chairs with pillows and light blankets, with Charles or I reading aloud to them from *Babar* or *Make Way for Ducklings,* while any dangerous weather wore itself out above our heads.

In the weeks before the three of us drove down to Woodberry Forest, Charles and I cordoned ourselves off from the rest of the world. It was my first experience—although I didn't recognize it as such—of being in the closet. Something in our lives might be ungenerously scrutinized, so we closed ourselves off from scrutiny by silence and isolation. Whatever we didn't talk about, or allow ourselves to consider, simply didn't bother us, and we managed to regain a certain peacefulness, enclosed as we were.

Without any of us realizing it, Stephen took charge of our entertainment, forsaking his own social life among his friends who were home from college and who called him regularly. Now and then he joined someone for a movie, but he was always home early, inquiring about our evening, about what we had done, what we were doing. And what we were doing was fairly strange, when I think of it.

I had tried to maintain an interest in a character from my second book—a child—whom I had been thinking about lately. She had become an adult in that part of my mind that is always engaged in another realm with its own timetable and population, and that is sometimes as real to me as my actual life. But she and all the people involved with her had literally become flat. When I conjured them up, they were strung across my imagination in rows like paper dolls.

The *New York Times Book Review* had asked me to do a long review of an enormous saga set in China and written by an author whose first book I had admired. I agreed to take it on, thinking that it was just the sort of distraction I needed, but my deadline was approaching, and I found I simply couldn't concentrate on reading or writing in the afternoons or evenings. Those have always been the most contemplative hours of any day for me.

Stephen usually came home to find us propped up in bed, where Charles pored over Amtrak timetables, although we weren't planning to go anywhere by train. I sat on the very edge of the other side of the bed, braced against pillows, with popcorn in a huge plastic garbage bag at my feet, which I was diligently—and with practiced and remarkable dexterity—stringing into long chains to hang on our Christmas tree.

"But, it's *May!*" Stephen said.

"These don't spoil. You can use them year after year. I'm just getting an early start." And I believed that was the reason I had strung enough popcorn chains to fill a second thirty-gallon plastic bag.

Charles, with schedules and notebooks spread across the bedspread, had figured out two-week, three-week, even month-long trips, with prices carefully noted and lodgings selected, to places we never planned to go, and I had made enough popcorn chains to bedeck every Christmas tree on our street, and yet it hadn't occurred to either of us that this was a form of crazy avoidance. We didn't even realize that it was such eccentric behavior that it might worry our son.

One night Stephen came in about ten o'clock with a bottle of wine and in a mood I have known since he was a child, a kind of ebullience that will brook no discouragement. "Come on," he said to us. "Come on! We have to get ready."

I only glanced up from my busy chain-making. "For what, sweetie? Get ready for what?"

"The meteor shower. There's going to be a meteor shower. Didn't you see it on the news?"

"Oh. We forgot to watch the news," I said.

"It's cloudy out tonight," Charles added.

Stephen was not deterred. "Oh, yeah. It's overcast right now, but it's supposed to clear. The clouds are already breaking up. I'm going to pull the hammock around to the side yard, out from under the trees. Where's the flashlight?"

Charles and I had grown so at ease with our fatigue—disinterest was such an easy retreat—that we weren't trying hard to shake it. "I don't think we have a flashlight that has any batteries in it. There might be one in the garage," Charles said.

"I'll see if I can find it. We can always use candles. I'll get everything set up."

We had no choice but to follow Stephen downstairs, although we tagged along dispiritedly, my long nightgown trailing beneath the hem of my robe, and Charles also in his robe, but wearing docksiders because he couldn't find his slippers. I had the uncomfortable feeling that some other people should be doing this. Glamorous people, who would have a robe and nightgown that matched, or—in Charles's case—would be wearing something other than a green terry cloth robe. I felt foolish.

Stephen preceded us with the only flashlight he had

been able to turn up, having cannibalized the radio for batteries, and we had to progress single file. Charles was carrying his and Stephen's wine glasses so that Stephen could navigate, and I followed Charles with my own glass and a second bottle tucked under my arm.

It was almost eleven o'clock on a weeknight in a town of fewer than eight thousand people, and the quality of the darkness was deep and inky. Our two German shepherds came around the corner of the house when they got wind of our procession, but at the sight of the beam of the flashlight, which apparently obscured our identity, they turned tail and retreated to the safety of the porch, silent and wary. Years earlier we had bought the dogs with the idea that they would be nice pets and excellent watchdogs, and now we all laughed at their cowardice and called their names to reassure them. I felt an ease and lightheartedness come over me that I realized was simple joy. We all felt it. We became silly with the effort of arranging ourselves sideways—three across—in the wide rope hammock without spilling our wine.

Stephen opened the second bottle, since we had sloshed most of the first over the ground as the hammock swung wildly when we climbed in. At last we leaned back comfortably and sipped our wine, gazing up at the sky in search of the spectacular light show Stephen had promised us. In fact, we never saw a single shooting star, although for a moment I became excited when I spied what might have been a meteor but was only an airplane overhead.

It was velvety quiet outside, with an amazing array of stars in constellations I could never discern, but which Stephen and Charles tried to point out to me. I didn't care that I couldn't see them; I was merely happy to be having a wonderful time. I thought that if we could just go get Jack and move to some unpopulated island where there would be no one from whom we would have to protect ourselves, no one to judge us or to wish us ill, then I could be content for the rest of my life.

I lay back in the hammock and watched the sky and listened to Stephen and Charles chatting and telling amusing stories to each other, and I was so pleased with my idea that I turned it into a fantasy. I wanted a craggy island, perhaps off the coast of Maine, that would have radical changes of climate with each season. I wanted quiet and books and dogs and cats and cable TV, and my husband and my two children. That would be the best way to live our lives, I thought. Everyone under one roof where I could protect them. We didn't need the encumbrance of a community, or of anyone who could withhold approval.

So there I was, delighted by the brilliant starlight, with the dogs nudging the hammock in excitement at having us outside so unexpectedly, and as I drank wine in the beautiful night, everything I imagined seemed absolutely reasonable, so preoccupied was I with the reconfiguration of our familiar calendar.

Chapter Three

Blind
Mice

I SPENT MOST OF THE SUMMER of 1987, before Jack's departure for his first year at Woodberry Forest School, searching out those things the school deemed essential—extra-long twin bed sheets, for example. I've wondered sometimes if summer camps and independent schools go out of their way to make lists of obscure or hard-to-find items that campers and students must bring along with them merely to keep parents occupied over the weeks before their child leaves home.

I made daylong trips to distant outlet stores in search of reasonably priced wool blankets—*two* of them, which made me wonder if they heated the school at all in the hills of Virginia. A window fan, lamps, a chair, a rug, towels, a bedspread. Jack wasn't much interested in collecting these things, so I was left to ponder alone what sort of rug would be acceptable to a first-year boy at a boarding school. It was up to me to figure out what kind of chair the school expected the family to furnish, and, in fact, I discovered on our first parents' weekend that Jack's roommate had arrived with a leather club chair replete with brass studs. It filled a quarter of their room, and the collapsible director's chair I had sent along with Jack was stored, folded, in his closet.

Meanwhile, though, I discovered an outlet in an old mill near Williamstown that sold seconds of various brands of domestic goods: bedding, towels, sheets, bedspreads, and even rugs. I was tired and sneezing and dust-covered, but nearly obsessed with the determination to find the rug that would ensure Jack's happiness and popularity and acceptance, that would transform a sterile dorm room into a place that would provide the sense of confident ease one feels only in one's own home. I was looking for exactly the right rug, but, of course, I was really in search of a magic carpet.

Opposite me across the nearly four-foot mound of stacked rugs was another shopper who was rapidly, and with a practiced flip of her wrist, turning the corners of the rugs back upon themselves, and making notations in a small notebook of the numbers pinned to the rugs in which she was interested. She was unusually dressed for outlet-browsing—a silk blouse elegantly scarf-draped, earrings, a handsome, chunky bracelet, a pretty, drifty, voile skirt. She possessed intimidating flair, and her efficiency was daunting; she seemed to know exactly what she was looking for and how to find it, and she interested me. It seemed to me that she might know where I could find just what I needed.

"It's dusty work, isn't it?" I said.

"Umm." She straightened and smiled a little in acknowledgment, brushing her hands together briskly to clean them. "The residue in some of these rugs can cause a rash. You ought to have these thoroughly cleaned before you put them down in your house."

"Well, actually I'm trying to find a rug for my son to take with him to boarding school. I just don't know what kind of rug to look for."

"These are *dhurries!* How old is he?"

"He's just fourteen. This will be his first year away."

She continued to flip through the corners of the rugs, making one more notation. "I can't imagine a fourteen-year-old boy wanting a dhurrie rug," she said with arch disapproval. "Why don't you get him one of those rugs with the school name or something . . . maybe the mascot printed on it. All those private schools sell rugs like that. That would be much more appropriate." I had irritated her in some way I couldn't fathom, and her voice dropped into a sort of honeyed acerbity. "You've got to loosen the apron strings, Mother."

I was astounded at her presumption, at the fact that she felt at liberty to insult me when I was an absolute stranger to her, at her implication that my interest in choosing a rug for Jack was somehow a little cute, a little foolish, and amusingly doting. I left the outlet, drove to a commercial carpet store, and bought a four-by-six beige polyester/wool carpet remnant. I thought about it carefully as I drove home and decided that surely a bound remnant—and beige, at that—would be neutral enough not to seem to have been foisted upon Jack by an overly protective mother.

When Jack left that September of 1987, to take up his first year of residency away from his own home, I didn't go along when Charles drove him down to Virginia, in part because the car was packed to overflowing, and in part because I knew it would make me sad—perhaps beyond disguising—to drive away from another school leaving a fourteen-year-old son behind. I stayed at home and paced the house, sat outside with the dogs, went out to dinner with a friend, and avoided Jack's room.

It was Jack's choice to go away to school, and I was very pleased for him when he was admitted to Woodberry, which was the only school to which he wanted to apply. But we live in an odd culture, I think. Letting children go is difficult, and it should be accomplished with as much grace as possible. Good behavior on the part of parents is essential for the sake of the child, but parents are supposed to *believe* that having their children leave home isn't a wrenching experience. I don't mean that it's unremittingly sad; I mean that it is an enormous change and is generally accompanied by curiosity and anticipation as well as inevitable sorrow. It seems to me that on this issue mothers, particularly, are routinely condescended to by all of society.

Little names are given to big adjustments: the "empty nest syndrome," for example. The connotations of that phrase—a carping, fussy, nagging sort of woman, a henpecked child—are inescapable and are never applied to men. I have never heard anyone suggest coyly to any grown man that he is suffering from the empty nest syndrome; I have never heard a father's grief so trivialized. When speaking about the behavior of men when their children leave home, people will often say, "Oh, yes, it hit him pretty hard." And the tone is somber and respectful and passive.

But women are reduced to the status of busy little birds. Who would want to be so categorized? Certainly not I; I was cheery to the point of mania as I sewed labels in Jack's clothes and inked his name on towels and sheets. Jack was uneasy, too, although he and I were prohibited by cultural expectations—and probably by our Wasp background—from ever discussing it. So the summer was filled with a kind of forced cheer and feigned indifference and unexpected, unexplained crankiness on all parts.

Charles and Jack timed their trip in order for Jack to be at the school the following morning when the other "new boys" arrived. Charles phoned me as soon as they checked into the Holiday Inn in Culpeper, Virginia, to let me know they had arrived safely. Jack sounded numb when I had him on the line. "What have I done to myself?" he asked.

I was nonplussed by the question, because he had articulated exactly what I had been wondering on my own behalf. But I did my part. I reminded him that he had become particularly fond of several faculty members at Woodberry when he had been at the summer session the previous year and that the talent and enthusiasm of those teachers were the reason he had chosen to go away to school. I talked about the beauty of the grounds and how close he would be to Charlottesville, Washington, even

Baltimore. I suggested that he and his father go out to a movie. I also said that if he needed to, if it didn't work out, he could always come home, and I think he was reassured that I had said so even though he rejected the idea as soon as it was put forward. He and I both knew that it was no longer I who could assuage his doubts, anyway. He knew where his father and I would be, and he knew that we would be fine; he was healthily anxious about how he would fare at his new school and whether or not he would like it.

Of course, I knew better than to make Jack responsible for the anxiety and sorrow I was feeling, or, in fact, even to let him know about it—it's an inevitable stage of family evolution. But I should have acknowledged it to myself. I should have felt free, in those two solitary days, to sit down and cry, and admit to myself that I felt an incalculable sense of loss. I knew how much I would miss Jack because of having gone through Stephen's leave-taking two years earlier, but no one had warned me that I would feel bereft when my younger and last child left home.

One morning in the first week of October of that same year, nearly five weeks since Jack had gone, everyone in the Berkshires awoke to an astonishing sight right outside their windows. A heavy, wet snow had fallen overnight and was still falling through the morning. The trees were in full leaf; most had not yet changed color. The huge old lilac bushes between the porch and the driveway were splayed flat against the snowy yard, and the branches of the towering Norway spruce next to the driveway, of the stand of walnut trees in back of the house, even of the scrub honeysuckle that fill the wooded corner of the yard where the forest was never cleared—all the tall trees and even the broad, sturdy bushes—were flexed so deeply that they looked ill-formed.

We put on old clothes and our snow boots and went outside, just as our neighbors were doing, to try to shake off the snow and liberate the lower branches from some of their burden, but with little success. There was a loud snap in the distance as Charles and I struggled to shake the snow off evergreen branches that were threatening to knock over our fence, but I didn't pay any attention until I heard a series of what seemed to be gunshots in the distance. We were in back of our house by the open meadow, and we both instinctively ducked low to the ground, assuming that deer hunters were at large on the rising hills not so far from where we stood. But the reports increased to the level of rapid artillery fire, and the two of us just looked at each other blankly.

We couldn't imagine what we were hearing until the leafy, snow-burdened head of one of the three tall maples by the road in front of our house suddenly seemed to make a half turn upon its trunk and, with a loud creaking and then a sudden, resonant crack, tumbled slowly into the road. The branches sprang back after the tree hit the pavement so that the huge mass bounced and rolled, flinging snow in a wide arc as it finally came to rest. And then the tree next to it crashed slowly down, and in a few minutes there was chaos as the trees everywhere around us broke midway down their trunks, releasing their snow-heavy crowns, or—like the beautiful oak in the center of our yard—creaked, and flexed, and slowly split in two, the center giving way to the inexorable pull of the opposing branches. We retreated to the shelter of our porch and watched as all around us the shrubs and trees and high branches reached their breaking point.

It was horrible and compelling, and we stared out at our yard in awe. As the trees in the mountains fell at such a distance there was a shrill keening noise of their bending and then a final snap of giving way. Later that day our neighbor across the street, a serene woman, an avid gardener, sophisticated and not especially sentimental, stood with tears running down her face as we all gazed at the decimated neighborhood greenery and the forest beyond the meadow, and asked us if we had heard the trees screaming.

For months after that freakish early snowstorm I was taken aback whenever I caught sight of the torn and broken trees, their trunks split, raw, and bright orange-brown in the dark forests of the Berkshires, and I, too, would find myself moved to tears. Twice, when I was driving and caught sight of a broad, scarred, forested vista, I had to pull over and stop the car because I was caught by surprise in a paroxysm of sobbing. It's strange that I've only just realized what was happening to me; it was permissible and even safe to grieve this natural damage, this violent breaking away, and I think, now, that it was probably a relief.

BUT THE WEATHER WAS BEAUTIFUL in the Berkshires in late spring 1991, when Stephen and Charles and I set off early in the morning to go to Jack's graduation.

In light traffic it is a ten-hour drive from our doorstep to Woodberry Forest School, and at the end of the first week in June, Charles and Stephen and I were in good spirits as we packed the car for the drive to Virginia. I had been up late the night before finishing my review for the *New York Times* and had mailed it off by Express Mail as soon as the post office opened. I had just made the deadline and was taking a copy with me to edit at the Holiday Inn in Culpeper, Virginia, where we always stayed when we visited Woodberry. I made sandwiches and added them to the cooler along with small cans of V8 and apple juice, because Charles and I had made the trip often enough that we knew there was no decent place to stop for lunch.

The first leg of the trip was fine. Along the Taconic State Parkway the forests had almost entirely healed since that devastating snowstorm. Only occasionally was there a swath in the woods of downed trees, dead and brittle gray underbrush, and new-growth hardwood saplings, much vigorous, opportunistic sumac, and the silvered skeletons of large trees that had not survived but still stood, vine-draped and starkly sketched against the leafy background, startlingly beautiful in their own right.

It was pleasant being enclosed in our air-conditioned car driving through the rolling landscape of southern New York State. We had happened onto an FM radio station in the middle of its fund-raising drive. The earnest DJs were airing a program called "Songs for Aging Children," hoping, I suppose, to raise money from people about my age. It amounted to something of a Joni Mitchell fest, whose songs they played relentlessly, one after another, the lyrics as earnest and dated as the music. They introduced Richard Harris's "McArthur Park" with reverence.

"The cake," Stephen said. "What's that cake? Why is it raining on the cake? What's he talking about?"

"Oh, it was all so profound," I said. "Our music was important, wasn't it Charles? All that symbolism. Come on, Steve. Don't tell me 'McArthur Park' doesn't affect you deeply. Doesn't make you mourn the end of such a significant era?"

I can't imagine that the station raised much money from that program that day. All the songs were turgidly profound in a way I had forgotten: Joni Mitchell's insipid "Tin Angels." And Simon and Garfunkel, usually so whimsical, wasting Garfunkel's beautiful, boys' choir tenor in "The Sound of Silence."

We were fascinated and amused by the awfulness not only of having to listen to "Both Sides, Now," but of having to hear oddly humorless banter—the two hosts were lost in reverent admiration without a trace of irony as they introduced the song.

Stephen was incredulous. "You really listened to music like this? I mean this was popular? Seriously popular?"

"Give us a break," Charles said. "Besides, I remember some song that either you or Jack and your friends played constantly. About sixth, seventh grade? Something like "Wake Me Up Before You Go Go"? That awful song by George Michael. A far cry from Simon and Garfunkel."

"No one should be held responsible for anything they did when they were twelve years old, Dad. Besides, I never liked that song."

"*I* liked that song," I said. "It was bouncy."

But Charles countered. "Unh uh! Nope, Steve. I remember Duran Duran—"

"I *liked* Duran Duran. The video with the waterfall," I said.

None of my family has ever trusted my taste in popular music, and Charles went on, "I remember when you had a party and some kid played nothing but 'Reflex.'" And Charles sang a little of it in a consciously self-important seriousness:

> "*The reflex is an only child, he's waiting by the park*
> *The reflex is in charge of finding treasures in the dark and*
> *Watch over lucky clover, isn't that bizarre*
> *Every little thing the reflex does is an answer*
>   *with a question mark.*"

"I *liked* 'Reflex,'" I protested once more, but Charles was oblivious.

> "*So why-yi-yi-yi-yi don't you use it*
> *Try-yi-yi-yi-yi not to bruise it*
> *Buy-yi-yi-yi-yi time don't lose it.*"

Stephen mimicked the round, earnest tones of the patient adult-speaking-to-child voice that can be heard in nursery schools and grocery stores anywhere in the country, and all around the world for all I know. "Now, Dad. You have to behave yourself or I'm afraid you'll have to take a 'time-out.' If you don't calm down, I'll just have to turn this car around right now!"

We all laughed, but I was determined to make my point. "But you have to admit that was a great video, Charles. You do! The one with that waterfall. . . ."

We were comfortable through the whole first leg of the trip, chatting back and forth. By the time we pulled into the Sunoco station in Statlertown, Pennsylvania, where we always filled the car with gas and had our lunch at a picnic table under two trees at the rear of the lot, the temperature outside was about ninety degrees, although the humidity wasn't bad, and there was a breeze blowing. Stephen filled the car with gas and cleaned the windshield while I set out our modest picnic—peanut butter sandwiches, apples, and juice.

The picnic table at that particular service station sits on a bluff above a little motel of about twelve rooms that—over the previous four years—I had become convinced was the center of some kind of mildly illicit operation. It was about one in the afternoon, and, as usual, there were several pickup trucks and a van backed up to some of the rooms of the one-story building, with young men loading and unloading large boxes. Boxes that approximated the size of VCRs, microwaves, TVs, small electronics. Two of the pickups were pulled up next to each other with their hoods up, and the drivers had connected cables so they could jump-start the battery of one of their trucks.

Over the years that Jack was away at school I had become intrigued with this slightly seedy strip of real estate in Statlertown. Sometimes when I felt particularly overwhelmed with the effort of getting my writing done while also living a real life, I would think to myself that I could always go to that little motel, because even though it seemed to me that something illegal might be going on, the perpetrators seemed to be a good-natured bunch. As odd as this sounds, I've discovered that this fantasy of uninvolved anonymity is pretty common among women, and maybe particularly among women who write. The two men working on the trucks were also talking about a good place to fish for bass. The door of the room in which they had unloaded the boxes was open behind them, and it was sparsely furnished but looked clean.

I had unpacked our lunch and was sitting at the table wondering what sort of job I could get in Statlertown if I ever were to relocate there. Charles had disappeared into the men's room, and I didn't realize that Stephen was sitting at the other end of the table until he spoke.

"Aren't you going to have any lunch?" he said, startling me. "It's windy. A bunch of the napkins blew away."

"There's some Kleenex in the car. I'll have a sandwich. Thanks."

He sorted through the sandwiches in the cooler. "They're all peanut butter. Is that okay?"

"Sure. That's all I packed. They don't spoil."

We each sat eating our sandwiches with one hand and holding down our napkins and V8 cans with the other because the breeze was so strong. Stephen was grinning to himself, and I was curious. "What? Why are you smiling?"

"No reason." But he tried to stifle an actual laugh.

"What? That's not fair. You have to tell me."

"I was just thinking about those peanut butter sandwiches you used to pack for me and Jack to take to school." And he did laugh out loud, a real laugh, and Stephen's laugh is infectious, so I laughed, too, but I didn't know why.

"Why is that funny?"

"It's not," but he was still smiling. "It's just that they were peanut butter, too."

"I thought you liked peanut butter. Anything else would have spoiled in your lunch box."

"I know. No, they were fine. It's just that you made them every month. I mean, all at once."

This was true. I had found the idea in a newspaper article entitled "The Creative Lunchbox." It was one of the author's least creative suggestions, but the most helpful. She had explained that sandwiches could be prepared and stored in the freezer as much as a month in advance, popped frozen into a lunchbox, and by noon they would be thawed and fresh even in hot weather.

"That was so they would be cool when you ate them."

Stephen laughed. "They weren't cool."

"What do you mean they weren't cool? Do you mean that it wasn't a cool thing to do? Did people make fun of your *sandwiches?*"

Stephen was laughing helplessly by now, trying to

explain, but I was no longer amused. This interfered with my idea of myself as my children's mother.

"Steve! What was wrong with your sandwiches? I packed those sandwiches for you and Jack for five years! Neither of you ever said anything about it."

"No," he said, suppressing laughter. "Really, they were fine. There was other stuff in our lunch. We always had granola bars and an apple or something."

"But, Stephen! Why did you need other stuff? What was wrong with the sandwiches?" I had put my own sandwich aside. My curiosity was in dead earnest.

"It wasn't a big deal. Really." And he was grinning at the memory. "It's just that when we unwrapped them, they were just this sort of soggy purple all over. Kind of spongelike. I guess the jelly soaked through, or something."

I was appalled. "What do you *mean?* How did you eat them? Why didn't you *tell* me?"

"Mom, kids don't care about their lunches. Craig used to pay someone to eat his apple, because his mother made him bring the core home to prove he had eaten it. Nobody had good lunches. We didn't want to hurt your feelings. We had plenty to eat at lunch. Sometimes the sandwiches were fine. Probably that just happened when it was hot."

"But that was the point. . . ."

This was absurd. I was moved to a state of terrible distress by the fact that my children had been stuck with soggy sandwiches for lunch for years of their lives.

The first year that both my children were away at school I had had a dream that I had never mentioned to anyone. In my dream I had been delighted to be going to my first day of work in a bank. My employer ushered me through the building and down many flights of stairs until we came to a room lit only with fluorescent lighting. He showed me to a cubicle very like my French language lab in the seventh grade. Then he went away, and a wonderful peacefulness came over me as I arranged my pencils and paper, paper clips and notepads. I was content. But suddenly the man reappeared, rolling ahead of him a two-tiered stainless steel surgical cart. The lower shelf was filled with loaves of Wonder Bread in their bright wrappers, and on top of the table were industrial-sized jars of Jiffy Peanut Butter and Welch's Grape Jelly.

"Our cafeteria has broken," he said to me, "and we need you to make lunch for the rest of the people in the building."

And then in my dream I was alone with the surgical cart, wondering whether to do all the peanut butter sides first, and then the jelly, or if it would be better to do each sandwich one at a time.

I woke up in a terrible state, feeling overwhelmed with dread, and uncertain for a few minutes whether I had dreamed all that or whether it had actually happened. I had always thought that it was such a silly dream that it would be embarrassing to mention it to anyone, and yet I had remained hung over with the anxiety of it for days.

The truth was that when my children were young I had hated leaping out of bed, fixing breakfast, and making school lunches. Since they had been away at boarding school I had my mornings to myself, even to sleep late if I liked. Other than their own pleasures and triumphs at their separate schools, it was one of the few delights I had taken in their being away from home.

I knew I had made large mistakes in my life as a parent. I had spoken words that could never be unsaid; I had been away teaching during important times in my children's lives; I had sometimes failed to take their interests properly into account. It is hard to be anyone's child; there's no way out without being wounded to some extent. The best you can do as a parent is to try to recognize and make amends for the mistakes you do make, any pain you do cause.

But sitting at that picnic table in Statlertown, Pennsylvania, I really and truly was deeply wounded. I was hurt that Stephen didn't understand the desperation of mothers, and I was terribly upset that not only had he not admired my ingenuity, he had suffered from it. And I also wondered if I had failed to disguise my resentment of my own children at six o'clock in the morning. I wondered if they had realized how tired and angry I was to be fixing their breakfast and their lunch at dawn, and if they had dangerously internalized my exhausted nurturing in those early hours. There's almost no end to the ways mothers can blame and martyr themselves: I was trying out a scenario in which coping with frozen peanut butter and jelly sandwiches had made Stephen decide to give up women and become gay.

My mood plummeted when we were back on the road, and it was contagious. By the time we reached Harrisburg and picked up U.S. Highway 15, we all began to feel uneasy; conversation lagged, and I don't think that any of us understood why. The three of us had lived together for nearly four weeks in a state of protected and exquisite isolation, but now we were moving inexorably into the real world, back into society.

And as we drove farther south, I was also lost in a morass of conjecture about the past. Despite Stephen's ideas to the contrary, was there something Charles and I had done or not done as parents that might have caused Stephen to choose his sexual orientation? He had seemed baffled and amazed by that very question when I had asked it as we sat on the porch almost four weeks earlier. It seemed to me that if he had chosen to be gay then it was not the idea of choice that our society would recognize. But in some way unfathomable to us had we forced him into a desire for a kind of love that would make his life difficult and even dangerous? That would possibly make him a pariah? Had he ever been so mutable?

He was born in Charlottesville, Virginia, in 1971, when Charles was a visiting professor at the University of Virginia. Stephen was in a breech position when I arrived at the hospital in labor, and in case they had to give me an anesthetic in order to perform a cesarean, I wasn't given any food or water for over sixteen hours. The last thing on my mind was any thought of eating, but I have never been so thirsty in my life. When I resorted to absolute and craven supplication for just a little *sip* of water, a nurse gave me a damp washcloth to suck on. I wasn't in the least bothered by such an indignity. In fact, I can't remember any moment in my existence when my concentration was as distracted as it was then by that desperate thirst.

I had opted for "natural childbirth," so I was awake

and alert through Stephen's delivery, but I found the Lamaze technique didn't really do me much good after the first six hours or so, except that I *did* know what was going on and that I wasn't likely to die from it. I had a long labor, and by the time Stephen was born I was unable to connect any of what had happened to me with a baby. It merely seemed to have been an interminable state of discomfort and pain from which I had finally, and literally, been delivered.

In the delivery room, though, I could tell from the attitude of my doctor and the nurses that at that moment it would be some sort of betrayal of basic human etiquette if I didn't adequately appreciate this first moment of motherhood. When the doctor gave the baby to me, I tried to behave as I was clearly expected to behave: I expressed amazement and delight and declared that this was the most wonderful moment of my life. The delivery room personnel whisked Stephen away for procedures that they began to explain to me, but I was impatient. I had fulfilled all the expectations I could handle for the time being.

I asked—no, begged—for a glass of water. I envisioned it filled to the brim with crushed ice. It was the thought of that ice—that almost-soft, hospital crushed ice, not brittle squares, but varisized rounded nuggets, slightly yielding between the teeth, cold and wetly melting—that induced, finally, an almost heartbroken weeping on my part.

My doctor misinterpreted my distress and assured me that the baby would be returned to me as soon as I was settled in my own room. But I wept on, unable to persuade anyone to bring me some water. The assembled medical personnel apparently concluded that I was in a sort of hysterical ecstasy, and therefore I more than satisfied their yearning for an appropriate reaction from a new mother.

At last, when I was in a clean gown in a quiet hospital room, my genuine reaction to the fact of this baby was another matter altogether. I knew I hadn't done a very good job of *having* this child—about halfway through my labor I had insisted on going home. "I've changed my mind," I had said. "I've decided not to do this." I had become really nasty and foul-mouthed when the two nurses in the room with me had laughed. I hadn't meant to be funny; I had meant to get out of the whole situation, which had begun to seem interminable.

Charles and I had gone through two six-week sessions of Lamaze classes, and if all that work I had done in preparing myself to give birth had resulted in such a poor performance, how could I possibly believe that—in spite of all I had read—I would have any idea how to take care of an infant? The birth of this child was the most astonishing consequence of any action I had ever taken, but I couldn't grasp the whole idea. It was one of those moments when actual time moved beyond me, and I was disoriented.

Because he had been delivered in a breech position, Stephen's forehead was high and smooth, and he had large, dark eyes, beautifully long and widely almond-shaped, filled with what seemed to me uncanny awareness. When a nurse gave him over to me I held him cautiously; I felt shy under his scrutiny, and there was no doubt in my mind that he was sizing me up. When Charles came in a little later I handed the baby over to him. Stephen's attention was as fixed on his father's face as it had been on mine. And there was one thing that was clear to me from the beginning, even before I made a full leap into the overwhelming state of motherhood: it was immediately apparent that Stephen already possessed his own nature. It was clear to us and a little alarming, because we hadn't even thought about taking care of an infant who had a *personality*. That this child was already very much himself was a stunning revelation.

So I wondered, nineteen years later, as I leaned my head against the window and watched the pretty horse country of northern Virginia pass by, if it was possible that Charles and I had had the power during Stephen's childhood to shape his sexuality in any way other than it originally had been. The notion seemed absurd on the face of it, but it is an idea that exists in society, and I was insulted by the thought not only on Charles's and my behalf, but because it stripped Stephen of the fact of his autonomy, of ever having possessed his own inherent individuality.

The closer we got to Woodberry Forest School, the more uneasy Stephen and I were becoming. The solitary allegiance he and Charles and I had forged in Williamstown was fraying at the edges. My mind began to brood in forward motion, and I didn't quite allow myself to think about Stephen and Jack's trip to Mexico and what might happen there. I did my best to back away from all the stereotypes I had not known—and would not have believed—I had of gay men. But I don't think it is so uncommon for parents to imagine the most terrifying scenarios of any situation in which their children might find themselves. This was a more sophisticated version of feeling the sensation of a fall my young sons did not take, and I suppose I had to go through it.

I worked very hard not to think of all the dangers Stephen faced, but there I was, stuck with the popular and clichéd idea of the sexually predatory nature of gay men, of their supposed insatiability—of their *difference*. I know—or know about—the myriad and sometimes bizarre manifestations of heterosexual lust. However heterosexual sex is played out—whether one thing or another would interest or arouse me—it stems from a desire I understand. I had no frame of reference for homosexual desire. It had never occurred to me to imagine it, and my imagination failed me so utterly that I didn't even give a thought to the fact that it was bound to entail equal variety.

It's true that Stephen didn't seem to me to fit any stereotypical mold, but it's also true that parents really know nothing at all about their children's sex lives, almost to the same degree that children can't imagine their parents' sex lives. Even more to the point is that it was none of my business—it shouldn't have mattered. I didn't wonder any of this about Jack. And it was blatantly unfair that, when Stephen offered to answer any question I might ask, I hadn't had the courage to do anything to allay my misgivings. I thought it was possible that if I had asked questions, his answers might also have heightened my anxiety. I'm not sure whether any of this would have occurred to me if I hadn't also had to contend with our society's hatred of and violence against gays and lesbians, and if I hadn't been all too aware of the terrifying indomitability of the AIDS virus.

It would have been helpful to have known how many gay men and lesbians I was well acquainted with already, but who were closeted, then, and, unfortunately, remain publicly closeted today. The two gay men I had worked with closely were two of the most distinguished and admirable men I knew, but they were both much older than I, and I knew nothing at all about their personal lives. In fact, it wasn't they who told me they were gay, but I hadn't found out in the manner of snide gossip, either. These two men are widely respected, and I suppose it was simply as a matter of fact, of common knowledge, that I knew they were gay. In those early days I wish I had remembered to think to myself that Stephen might live his life as they did, because most dismaying of all was the thought that my son was involved in a game that had no rules. I no longer knew how to envision his future.

Also, I was becoming more and more distressed at the idea that Jack knew nothing of all this. Charles and Stephen had traded off driving just outside of Harrisburg, Pennsylvania, and Charles had made himself comfortable in the backseat and fallen asleep.

I looked at Stephen covertly as he was negotiating traffic, and I could see the tension he was feeling in the tightening of his jaw and the muscles of his neck. He had insisted that we get a decent bottle of champagne—rather than the bottle of Andre's I had bought—for the ceremonial and otherwise strictly forbidden glass that the Woodberry graduates always drank immediately following the graduation ceremony when they congregated on the lawn. Stephen thought it would be important, and he insisted that we at least buy a respectable brand even though it was going to be drunk mostly from the bottle, passed among friends.

I had made tentative arrangements at a restaurant near the school for a luncheon Charles and I wanted to host on the day before graduation for Jack and his closest friends from Woodberry and their families, whom Charles and I had gotten to know over the phone and at parents' weekends. Jack made it clear, though, that he would much prefer just to say his good-byes on his own, and Charles and I scaled down our plans. Both of us thought Jack had sounded burned-out on the phone, under pressure of final exams, and ready to be done with school. It was Stephen who reminded me to bring along the graduation presents I had bought for the boys I had assumed would be attending the luncheon, and we had had to double back on our way out of Williamstown to pick them up.

I believed that it was Stephen whom Jack would be most excited to see, and I knew he was most interested in having Stephen meet his friends and some of the faculty. Stephen probably thought so, too, and was even more tormented than I at being in a position in which he didn't think he should or could tell Jack a crucial thing about his life. Just then I felt so sad for both my sons.

A family is a complicated beast. Its definition is as elusive, really, as that of love, or joy, or art, or pornography—we can't define it, but we know it when we experience or see it. Family is a clumsy, bumbling sort of creature, lurching along through the decades, losing bits here and gaining them there. When I try to establish my idea of family, I always think of the Buddhist tale of the seven blind men asked to describe an elephant.

The first man, who felt the elephant's head, says it is like a large waterpot. The second man, who felt the elephant's ears, says it is like a flat basket. The third blind man, who has felt only the tusk, says it is like the sharp end of a plow; and the fourth man, who feels the elephant's trunk, says it is like a thick rope. The fifth man feels the elephant's back and body and thinks that it is like a crib full of wheat; the sixth man touches only the elephant's legs and declares that it is like four pillars; and the final blind man feels the elephant's tail and says that the beast is like a fan.

The parable is about the definition of God and that His nature cannot be inferred from individual experience, but I've always wondered about the elephant. In fact, that tale puzzles me, because it is agreed that each one of the seven blind men can only know a part of the elephant, but nowhere in the tale is there recognition of the fact that however the elephant is perceived by others, the *elephant* isn't puzzled. It doesn't question what it's like, and I've come to think that a family is much the same. Perhaps that elephant and any family can be recognized by its single heart. I'm well aware that it may not always be a good thing that there is something at the very core of a family that unites all its disparate factions. It is true, though, that a family may be divided internally, but, when threatened from outside, it will align itself in solidarity against assault. Publicly divided groups of people who may be related, may be siblings or parents and children involved in open dispute, really don't fit my definition of family.

But our family was still staggering with the shock of the assault; we weren't settled into any pattern yet. We hadn't attained the serenity of the elephant; we were as scattered as the three blind mice. Even so, Stephen must have known by the time we departed for Virginia that Charles and I—in however blundering a fashion—were ready to close ranks with him, but none of us knew what Jack would do or how he would feel. We did know, however, that without him we would no longer be a family.

In the past few weeks the three of us had spent together, the whole idea of the adherence of our family had taken on a conspiratorial quality, because without ever acknowledging it to each other, the three of us—and Stephen most of all—were aware that we were no longer the people our acquaintances thought we were. Charles and I did know that if society would cast one of us aside—scorn, deride, disapprove of, or censure any one of us—then each one of us would be equally injured. But Jack hadn't yet been included in our conspiracy, and now that we were finally going to see him again, the stakes were high. If the fact of Stephen's being gay separated the two brothers, our family would be forever hobbled.

By the time we were on the outskirts of Culpeper, I was rattled and apprehensive with the various imagined disasters I had thought of but not articulated, and I think Stephen was as uneasy as I. We were coming into light traffic, and he snapped at me as I applied my foot to my own imaginary brake on my side of the car in an involuntary, sympathetic response and tightened my grip on the arm rest.

"Do you want to drive?" he said, making only a semblance of an effort to keep the irritation out of his voice.

"No, Steve. I just think you're coming up to these stop lights awfully fast." The look of irritation on his face remained, but he didn't say anything else. "I just think your foot's a little heavy on the accelerator."

"I'm not even doing the speed limit. It's not great driving with you sitting next to me flinching every time we come to a light or I pass a car."

"Well, I can't help it. You may be driving under the speed limit, but it feels too fast to me."

"Ah, look at that," Charles said from the backseat. "There's a sign that says we've just entered Culpeper." He didn't sound tense. "Now, not many outsiders know this," he continued, on a jovial, confidential note, "but only tourists pronounce it *Cul-pepper*."

In the front seat the two of us relaxed a little, and Stephen took up the bantering with relief. "Tourists? Do they have tourists here?"

"Well, *outsiders,* then. Or newcomers," Charles drawled, playing up the local accent that he knew so well from having gone to school at Woodberry himself nearly forty years before, and from his recent trips to meet with the board of trustees. "Locally, if you've been here any time at all, you know it's pronounced *Cul-p'pa.* New boys never know about this. They're likely to go around saying 'I'm having supper in Cul*pepper*.' When the right way to say it is, 'I'm havin su-p'pa in Cul-p-pa.'"

Stephen and I laughed, and Charles was encouraged. "I'm going to put some pe-p-pa on my su-p-pa in Cul-p-pa." He had broken the tension, and he could see that Stephen and I were far more amused than was warranted. Charles and Stephen got involved in directions to our motel.

I was disburdened all at once and soared right into a state of euphoria. I was overcome with a wave of intense gratitude at being connected to everyone in my family, and I could scarcely wait to see Jack again after almost five and a half months. He had applied for early decision to and been accepted by Wesleyan University, so for the next four years he would at least be closer to home. But besides that, the last time he had been home he had seemed amazingly sophisticated and mature to me, and I thought it was exciting, and it was time, for him to be done with the fairly structured environment of his all-male secondary school. For a little while I thought it would be a simple thing to enjoy and celebrate Jack's graduation.

Chapter Four

Like
Home

OR ALL MY SAYING THAT I could recognize my children even if I was blindfolded in a room full of people, I didn't recognize Jack when he passed by the window of our motel room at the Holiday Inn. After we had checked in, Stephen went to his room to shower and change clothes, and Charles went to a board meeting at the school, from which he returned with Jack in tow. I did look up as Jack passed the room, and I thought to myself that he must be a college student, probably the older brother of a Woodberry boy whose family had also arrived a few days early. But when I heard Charles call Jack's name and saw this tall boy with longish light brown hair turn back to our door, I was shocked.

Jack was at least three inches taller than he had been when I had seen him last. His hair, once wheat-colored, was more brown than blonde. His face was starkly defined, high cheek-boned, and elongated, with no trace of childhood about it. While Stephen has always had a look about him of my father's family, the Formans, Jack takes after the Ransoms, my mother's family. My mother has the greenest eyes I've ever seen, and my grandmother, Robb Reavill, had intensely blue eyes. Charles's eyes are hazel. For years Jack's eyes had been a combination of all three, a blue/hazel. But now his eyes—darkly lashed and slightly down-turned at the corners—took on elusive but intense shades of green or blue if the light shifted. With his once-blonde but now charcoal-dark brows, he took my breath away—I didn't gasp in surprise, but I swallowed my first words; I could only smile. He had a mysterious, smoky, saintly look; he was like a creature from a Renaissance painting. He gave me a hug but seemed slightly guarded.

"You look wonderful! You look so different! It's wonderful to see you!" I said. But he had changed so much I felt embarrassed around him, and awkward.

Outside, the heat was astonishing, and we went to dinner at the Davis Street Ordinary, which had been recommended by all sorts of people, but which wasn't air-conditioned. We were fairly comfortable as long as we didn't move very much or drink wine with dinner. The restaurant is a restored tavern, probably dating from the mid-1800s, and our waitress was dressed in a long, ruffled calico dress and a mobcap. If she had ever been good-natured, that nature was sorely tried by having to carry from table to table a huge blackboard with menu choices presumably written out earlier that day but which, by then, were smudged and hard to decipher. We asked to see the regular menu, but she was mute with irritation, merely gesturing with a flourish to the board she had propped on a chair, disdainful of our unworldliness. Theirs was a bistro idea gone banquet-size—elaborate entrées lavishly described on a blackboard that was as large as the wall-mounted chalkboards of my grammar school days.

On the other hand, her disdain for us had the happy effect of uniting us against the absurd formality of the restaurant and the obvious disapproval we elicited from the staff because of our relatively casual dress and our lack of appreciation for the refinements of the establishment. Jack and Stephen seemed to be comfortable with each other and amused.

Several times I caught myself gazing at Jack in wonder. I was unnerved by our all being together again, and I was simultaneously fighting sorrow. He was so old all of a sudden, and polite and distant in the way that your children become when they are really leaving. I had a desire to embrace him and implore him to stay, not to leave us this soon, to admonish him that he hadn't warned us to expect him to have changed so much. We hadn't come to Virginia prepared for his departure from our lives, and I knew instinctively that was what we were facing. But, of course, decorum prevailed as it did among all the other families of graduates I surreptitiously studied where they sat at other tables that evening and during the various ceremonies and formalities over the next few days.

He and Stephen dropped us off at the motel so that the two of them could go back to Woodberry and visit with some of Jack's friends. I was both reassured and alarmed seeing them together again. They seemed to like each other, and any parent knows how lucky that is between or among siblings. But I didn't know when Stephen planned to come out to Jack, and I agonized over their possible alienation.

WHENEVER I AM REALLY ANXIOUS for the welfare of someone I care about—safe trips of people I love, good health for someone in the hospital, and so forth—I wear a pair of opal and silver earrings that my children gave me for my thirty-third birthday, and not once have those earrings failed me. They're not beautiful—they are just very plain small studs—but no bad things, and many good things, have happened to the people on whose behalf I have worn them. The day before we were to leave for Jack's graduation, though, they weren't in my jewelry box; they were nowhere to be found, and I searched the house thoroughly and with increasing panic. Those opal earrings misplaced at just this time seemed to me to be a particularly bad omen, and when I finally gave up the hunt, I decided that the only thing to do was to find replacements.

There are drawbacks to living in a small town, and I ran headlong into one the day I was in search of opal earrings. In Williamstown there are several fine jewelers, but most trade in individual pieces made by talented designers across the country. There are no big stores like a Macy's, or even Sears, which would have had racks of mass-market but adequate opal earrings.

I finally ended up forty-five miles away in a little shop in West Stockbridge, Massachusetts. The more elusive a pair of opal earrings had become, the more convinced I was that if I didn't find any, Jack's graduation would be ruined in some way. I didn't even want to consider in what way that might be.

The shop I finally found was fascinating. Inside a glass case were displayed a number of Native American quilled boxes, which have interested me since I received a remarkable box as a gift from a couple who are two of my most cherished friends. No one appeared to be in the store as I studied the boxes, all of them oval, like mine, but none as intricately designed or nearly as beautiful.

Finally a woman came into the front of the shop from somewhere in the back. She was dressed in loose, flowing trousers, a mid-calf-length, batwing, brown and cream-colored tunic, and stunning jewelry that was dramatic and exotic. I was caught off guard. Under other circumstances I wouldn't have trusted the glamour she affected in this rural corner of Massachusetts.

"May I help you?" she said.

"I need a pair of opal earrings."

She glanced over the cases of jewelry, trailing the tips of her fingers along the chrome edges of the counters as she moved along and inventoried their contents. She paused, finally sliding back a glass panel in order to remove several pairs of earrings. "I don't believe I have any made up right now," she said. "But what about these? These are very handsome. They're cabochon clips. They have the same effect. A kind of luster."

"Oh no. Thank you. But I really *need* opals." I recognized too late that my tone was embarrassingly urgent for the occasion, and she stood back a moment and regarded me.

"Were you born in October?" she asked.

I nodded. "It's my birthstone. . . " I intended to try to explain the situation to her, but she held up her hand to indicate it wasn't necessary, and turned to a bank of little drawers that made up the inside base of the glass display cases. She took a loop of keys from her pocket, unlocked one of the drawers, and withdrew a tiny drawstring bag and handed it to me.

"Take these for the time being," she said, "and we can have earrings made up for you when my designer comes in."

I opened the bag and discovered perhaps fifty opals, smoothed and rounded and opaque. They glistened as I shifted the bag in my palm. "I can't take these," I said, although she was nodding that I should. "No, really. I can't take these. Not unless you let me buy them."

"Of course you can take them. You're welcome to take them if you need them. We can make up any sort of earrings you want when you bring them back."

I left the shop with the opals in hand, and when we returned from Virginia, I drove back to West Stockbridge but found the shop closed, although it was a weekday. I hadn't even thought to note the name of the store when I had first discovered it, so I wrote it down and drove home. The following week I tried to get the number from directory assistance, but they had no listing. I assumed the phone was in the woman's name, which I didn't know. I drove back to West Stockbridge to find the store closed once again, and twice more I returned, finally to find it closed and empty and for lease. But I'm saving those opals; I've kept them in their pale-blue chamois cloth bag, and they are ready to be returned at any moment to that woman in the batwing tunic.

I've saved all but the ones I gave to the young daughters of the couple who once gave me the extraordinary quilled box, which is now the repository for that little blue bag—extra double good luck! Although, if push comes to shove, I will swear that I'm not really superstitious. It's just that it seems to me that there are some ways to convince yourself—to remind yourself—that more often than not there are benign consequences to the inevitable and various events in any lifetime. If I ever find that jewelry shop owner I will reimburse her for the stones that are missing, because I do believe you can borrow a little luck now and then, but you can never steal it. I kept that cache of opals tucked inside my purse the whole time we were in Virginia.

When Stephen returned that evening from Woodberry and dropped by our room to say good night, I pressed him to find out if he had told Jack that he was gay, and he was patient, but he seemed pained at the question.

"I'll let you know when I tell him. Jack's just about to graduate. His friends seem great, but Jack would have been worried about having me meet them right now if I had told him I was gay."

"How do you mean?" I asked. I hesitated, wanting to know exactly what to expect. "Were you attracted to them, Steve? Is that what you mean?"

Stephen has an expressive face. I used to believe that he couldn't ever have gotten away with not telling the truth, and he isn't any good at it for run-of-the-mill sorts of situations. But, of course, I've realized by now that much of the energy of his life has been taken up with an elaborate kind of deception that he believed was necessary for his survival and to retain our approval. When I asked him this question, however, he looked angry.

"Why would you *ask* me that? It's none of your business! How would you feel if I asked *you* if you were attracted to Jack's friends? Or his teachers?"

A nice person would never have asked the question I had asked Stephen, and an enlightened person would have known that Stephen's attraction to or lack of interest in those young men who were Jack's friends was as beside the point as if he had been attracted to those young men's sisters. But I was far from enlightened; I had come to terms with only the *news* of Stephen's being gay, not the actuality. I was afraid of society, and I know now that I was counting on Stephen to make the situation easy for me at his expense—something he had done automatically for most of the years of his life.

And I have always known that when something matters to me very much I am not at all nice; I am selfish and ruthless and sometimes unintentionally mean. I felt sick at having invaded the privacy of my own son, but I was also terrified about his upcoming trip to Mexico, about the nature of his desire, because I was so ignorant. The really fine contemporary fiction by gay authors like David Leavitt, Michael Cunningham, Blanche McCrary Boyd, Dorothy Allison, and a host of other writers, has the attributes of all really fine fiction—it is unique and individual, and it hadn't even occurred to me to infer generalities from it. I had latched on to tabloid stereotypes and the most exaggerated and sensational of Tennessee Williams's plays, and I had been plagued by a performance of one of the last of the '60s poets, famously homosexual, who had launched into a tribute to sex with young boys. I hadn't thought to balance that out with—say—Nabokov and *Lolita,* or any of the number of straight male writers who implicitly or explicitly, and unabashedly, explore the terrain of the desire of grown men for young girls.

"Well, I *don't* know anything about this, Steve. I don't know . . . I mean, are you interested in young boys? I keep reading about these priests—"

He was hugely angry when he replied, although I could only hear it in his inflection. I know now how terrible it is that he didn't feel he had a right to be enraged. He must have given up long ago on the idea of there being any refuge from misconception in society at large, but he should not have had to allow one of his parents to fall into the trap of mistaking homosexuality for pedophilia. It's terrible that he thought he had to tread so carefully, and it's my fault, but it's not only my fault.

"You compare me to a mass murderer. You think that I might be a pedophile. But you've known me all my *life.* I've always thought you both were really good parents. That you understood a lot. I can't believe you'd ask me something like that. No." He stopped me as I began to explain and protest. "No. I can't believe you'd think of me like that. I'm just *gay.* Don't you even remember what you *used* to know about me? Well, it's not different!

You wouldn't ever have asked me if I was interested in little girls. Would you have ever asked me that? I'm no *different!*"

It must seem bizarre that a parent would injure her own child in such a way—a parent who claims to love that child. It may be that it's hard for people without children to understand much about parents at all. Months later, seeking advice about an unrelated local issue from a gay man who is a friend, I said to him in the course of the conversation that, naturally, if people in Williamstown withdrew their friendship from Stephen, then we would simply move somewhere else.

"Why would you do that?" he asked, genuinely puzzled. "Stephen isn't going to be *living* in Williamstown." I realized our experiences were so different that without enormous interest and effort on both our parts, I probably couldn't adequately explain it to him, and it wasn't the point of our conversation in any case.

But when I said the same thing to my doctor who is also a friend of sorts, and who has three children of her own, she said, "Of course. You would have to leave. Otherwise you would be betraying your own son." She was matter-of-fact, and I was relieved to find that my instinct wasn't entirely overwrought.

In that motel room in Virginia, though, Stephen and I were sitting across from each other separated only by a small table, but I thought it was possible that I had created such an abyss between us that it might never be breached. I don't remember if Charles was in the room, but I doubt it. He would never have asked such a question. I am the villain of our family, and either of my sons can tell you that, although they're kind and are likely not to be so frank. But I'm not sure that Charles didn't have the same anxieties, the same misconceptions. It's just that he would never have thought it was his business to ask, and he's right. He would never have infringed on Stephen's dignity, but he would have wondered and worried privately, and I simply don't possess the fortitude to do that. I'm not proud of it, but in this instance I couldn't overcome my own panic.

At that point I hadn't progressed past the stage of becoming teary when I looked at wedding pictures in the newspaper and thinking that I would never be part of an occasion like that, since Jack had said for years that he never wanted to get married. Birth announcements arriving in the mail threw me into despair. As much as I loved Stephen, I hadn't progressed past *me*. I was still involved in self-pity, and I was also scared. I needed to know as much as Stephen would tell me about what I thought of as the new version of him. It came down to the fact that it was unbearable to live within the little cocoon of my own ignorance, and I had only Stephen as a source of information. I wanted to be able to consider the future, to imagine our lives and how they would progress. I was distraught, myself, at the person I had become, and I began to cry.

"I don't know *anything*, Steve. I'm just scared to death. I'm scared that Jack seems so grown-up and remote. I'm scared for you. About what could happen to you. We're only *older* than you." This last statement was a plea, and I looked up and wiped my eyes, and hoped that Stephen would understand, but he still looked angry and shocked. "We're older," I said again. "We don't know any more about your life. . . . We can't know anything about what you want. . . ." I was so tired all at once that I was tempted to lean my head back against the chair and go fast asleep—to sink immediately into oblivion. "You only know us as your parents. You have a right to think we'll know exactly what you're like. I thought we *did* know exactly what you were like and exactly what Jack is like. But, God! We don't know a damn thing. All we know is that we love you both. We really love you both."

Stephen's face took on an expression of skepticism, and he seemed as fatigued as I felt. He rose from his chair and turned to me, and began to tick off items on his fingers as he relayed them in a calm, matter-of-fact, almost singsong voice. "Okay, Mom. It wouldn't have crossed my mind to think of Jack's friends as anything but Jack's friends. I've been involved with someone—with one person—for the past year. I think I would really like to be a parent someday, but that's my *only* interest in children. And I don't understand how you can wonder if I'm sexually interested in children and then tell me how much you and Dad love me."

I must have said something, but I don't remember what it was. I hope and imagine it was an apology. But I do remember thinking that children really don't know about parental love. I happen not only to approve of my children but also to admire them; that approval and admiration has nothing to do, however, with how much I love them.

On his way toward the door Stephen bent down and

gave me a quick embrace. It was one of several times in the past two years when I've marveled that I have two sons who are so generously compassionate.

Stephen and I had a late breakfast in the Holiday Inn restaurant the next morning, because Charles had left very early so he could meet with the board of trustees, who were convening in Washington, and Jack was busy at school until late afternoon. Charles was gone when I woke up, and I showered and got dressed feeling queasy with anxiety about seeing Stephen after the things I had said to him the night before. But when he knocked at the door he was in a good mood, and all through breakfast he was cheerful.

I kept apologizing discreetly. That was still a time when I would have been embarrassed if I thought our discussion might be overheard and understood by anyone else in the room—the waitress refilling our coffee cups, the couple sitting across from us side by side at a leatherette banquette. I don't think that I ever thought homosexuality, itself, was bad or wrong. I don't think I had considered it one way or another—it hadn't occurred to me that I had anything riding on an opinion. But I must have been afraid of the disapproval that might be incurred by the discussion or admission of it. I would prefer that people like me rather than not, but I want everyone to love my children.

"Don't worry about it, Mom," Stephen said. "I told you to ask me anything you wanted to know. I shouldn't have gotten upset when you did. I always thought you and Dad would be pretty good about this."

This silenced me completely, and relieved me enormously, but also left me puzzled. If my blundering around in the most intimate issues of my son's life could be considered being "pretty good about this," then what could entail *not* being good about it? Only once before in my life as a parent, when Jack and I had been really mad at each other, and I had said a terrible thing to him that I could never unsay but that I had never, never meant— only then had I been as ashamed of myself. That's such an easy phrase, and usually not at all sincerely tossed off. But I mean it absolutely. I was sick with shame, and, as in my argument with Jack, no amount of forgiveness or tolerance would completely alleviate my dismay at my own behavior.

My mother has always had a theory about autobiographies: she doesn't believe them, because she thinks that people are never likely to tell you the thing about themselves that they are most pleased with or that they are most ashamed of. I agree with her in general, but not in this case. So far in my life, the worst things I have done are having hurt my children in ways that I can never undo. But there are things I like about myself, too, and I do know that I have often been a good parent.

We ate breakfast without much conversation for a while, but in light of Stephen's remarkably good nature that morning, I finally dared another question that had tantalized me in wakeful moments all through the night. "Steve, I know you probably don't want to talk about the person you said you've been involved with. I know it's none of my business, and I realize I've taken a lot of liberties, anyway, with your private life. But is he a nice person? Well, I mean, does he come from a nice family?" I have no idea, in retrospect, exactly what I had in mind as a *nice* family, and Stephen slumped back in his chair and at first looked exasperated, and then he smiled a little.

"Yeah. I guess so. I wouldn't be involved with him if I didn't think he was *nice,* Mom. And his family's pretty nice. They're nice people. I think you'd like them," he said, and then he adopted an expression of mock doubt and a self-consciously cautious tone. "I *think* you'd like them, but . . . well . . . " He seemed hesitant to say more, but then he dropped his voice and leaned forward conspiratorially. "I *think* you'd like them. They're pretty respectable. But, I don't know. One of their children is gay."

I felt my face take on exactly the wide-eyed expression of surprise that Stephen had been coaxing from me, and then I began to choke on the sip of juice I had just taken, and to cough and . . . giggle—I don't know what else to call it. The silliness of the whole situation hit me: our elaborate courtesy, Charles's and Stephen's and my careful treading on eggshells, the arbitrary approbation of society, the ludicrous hierarchy of the social order. For a minute or so of helpless and stifled laughter I saw our lives in their proper perspective.

We had arrived three days early so that Charles could meet with the board to finish the process of selecting a new headmaster to replace Emmett Wright, who was retiring. I had to spend most of that day on the phone with an editor of the *New York Times Book Review,* getting my review in order, because I had been too distracted to rewrite it before we left. Jack was involved at school, and Stephen went to meet him for lunch and go into Charlottesville.

But earlier, as Stephen and I made our way along the sidewalks of the motel after breakfast, I had stopped to pick a magnolia from one of the three tall trees that screened the restaurant from the pool. I broke off a blossom that had not yet opened and put it in water in a glass in my room. The scent of a magnolia isn't sweet, although having been away from the South for so long I had forgotten that. I had imagined that it would have as heavy a perfume as a gardenia. But magnolias have a scent that is cool and a little peppery, lightly pungent.

All day as I worked on my review and discussed changes with my editor over the phone, the remarkable, nearly translucent petals loosened in a slow process of falling open. The magnolia's pale color—not white, but not exactly cream—and its articulated delicacy in spite of its size, were as beautiful, and even as faintly alarming, as the sight of the luna moth that had once alighted on my window screen when I was a child in Baton Rouge. While I wrestled with shortening my review, the flower engaged my interest, piqued my curiosity, entertained me now and then with the pleasure of looking at it, as nothing else had done in weeks.

But the next few days were strained. Jack's advisor, Daniel Elgin, and his wife, Maureen, joined us for dinner at the school, sneaking us past the crowd at the main door of the dining-room and spiriting us in the back way, to the outrage of the dining-hall attendants. My husband had come to rely on Daniel in his capacity as liaison between the board of trustees and the faculty, and to respect him as much as Charles had ever admired or respected any of his own colleagues and good friends. Daniel had been Jack's advisor for the whole four years at Woodberry, and Jack thinks he might not have stayed at the school through those first two years without Daniel on hand, not only as an advisor but as a brilliant teacher and, along with several other faculty members, a much needed counterpoint to a primarily conservative faculty and an almost entirely conservative student body.

At dinner I was sitting with Daniel's wife and finally getting a chance to know her in person rather than only through the various occasions she had received worried or celebratory or merely information-gathering calls from me over the phone. She is a wonderful person.

Daniel leaned across Charles to ask me what I thought of the change in Jack, and I was surprised to find that I sounded snappish. "Nervous and shocked," I said to him, and I realized I had surprised him. But Jack had gone through such a thorough metamorphosis that it seemed to me Daniel should have let us know. On the other hand, Daniel Elgin has seen hundreds of boys arrive at Woodberry Forest School at age fourteen and take their leave as different creatures four years later.

The morning of graduation was unseasonably hot. By 10:00 A.M., when we were all gathered on the lawn in front of The Residence—a serenely unpretentious but beautiful brick building purportedly designed by Thomas Jefferson—it was already over one hundred degrees. Small children in nice clothes had climbed down the temporary bleachers to lie flat on their backs on the ground, splayed out like starfish on the dark green lawn, and grown-ups stepped over them matter-of-factly. Paper cups of lemonade were passed out by dining hall attendants, and all among the crowd, people used their programs to fan themselves as discreetly as possible while we waited for the graduation procession to begin.

Behind and above me in the stands an exhausted woman tried to calm two small children who appeared feverish with the heat. At last she helped the little girl, who couldn't have been more than four years old, take off her wilted dotted swiss dress with its colored piping and tightly banded sleeves. The child slumped with relief into the woman's lap, wearing a perfectly modest camisole, but her brother was inconsolable, and every time he changed position in an effort to be comfortable, he sloshed lemonade down my back. I didn't mind the lemonade, but when the sun breached the tall oaks and bore down on those of us in the stands, I left Charles and Stephen and found shelter under the natural umbrella of a fir tree that all by itself generated a sort of cooling system. Another couple joined me, the woman slipping off her shoes and sinking into the cool blanket of needles beneath the tree.

At last the faculty marched across the lawn two abreast in a procession that stopped and parted to form an aisle through which the graduating class would pass. The heat was so distracting that I was surprised to find myself moved to tears when I caught sight of Jack making his way through the double line of faculty. He glanced a smile at Pamela Albergotti, an early ally and friend of his among the faculty, at Leonard Harvey, one of the finest teachers anywhere in the world, at Marshal Gill, another inspired teacher and a talented writer, and a grin almost of conspiracy at Daniel Elgin.

Because of Charles's respect for these particular faculty members, he had agreed to serve on the board in spite of the time-consuming business of chairing the history department at Williams College, and the labor of love of finishing a book that had entailed twenty years of research and writing. Over the four years of getting to know them myself, and through Jack's reaction to them, I had come to respect, admire, care about and feel grateful to these people who reached out to shake Jack's hand or touch his shoulder as he passed by. A graduation is irresistibly moving. It's a demarcation that is altogether triumphant, but it is also shadowed by the inevitable melancholy that accompanies change.

After the speeches and awards and receiving their diplomas, the graduates broke ranks after the first, perfunctory, congratulations from the assembled guests. They headed for the yard where they congregated to drink champagne, at last, and licitly, on the grounds of the school.

Charles stayed to talk with Leonard Harvey, and Stephen and I went back to our car so Stephen could get the champagne we had left chilling on ice and join his brother. I sat in the car and poured iced tea from a thermos into a clear plastic cup, turned on the air conditioner, and took off my shoes. I was sitting there sipping the already tepid tea and feeling simultaneously elated and nostalgic when a father of one of Jack's good friends stopped at my window, which I rolled down. He reached in to give me a hug, and we laughed and congratulated each other.

"Casey won't be far from you, next year," he said. "He'll be at Trinity."

"I know. It's been one of the things I've been re-minding myself of every time I feel like crying."

He nodded. "It's like that, isn't it? They did a good job, our boys. They really did well." And he smiled but spoke with a hint of regret. These four years were all over. "I'd ask you for a sip of that, but I never touch it. But don't you go back to Massachusetts and forget about us! We'll stay in touch. Lanie got some good pictures of Jack. She'll send them to you. We won't say good-bye." And he squeezed my hand and then moved away, offering a final wave when he was a few yards distant. It was a few minutes before I realized that he must have thought I was sitting in the car in the air-conditioning at eleven-thirty in the morning sipping straight whiskey from my plastic cup.

I watched the families slowly collect themselves—sending the youngest as emissaries to round up the strays—and depart. They were all perfect, those families, with their tall sons at their center. Not one of those families could have the slightest complication in their lives as they hoisted duffel bags and sports equipment into the backs of their station wagons. They were June and Ward Cleaver, Ozzie and Harriet, the Brady Bunch. The only difference would be their soft southern accents. I watched all these handsome people with an increasing sense of separateness. They seemed foreign to me, or perhaps it's more accurate to say that I felt foreign among them. They seemed to me to possess that southern ease within any surroundings that I only remembered. I am southern, but I didn't feel at home in the company of these southerners.

When we were looking at independent schools for Stephen, if I had had any inkling of its aristocratic history or of the snobbish reputation from which St. Paul's School still suffers, I would probably have urged Stephen to look elsewhere. St. Paul's did absolutely nothing to acknowledge that among their student body there were gay or lesbian students. But it is impossible to be on the St. Paul's campus for long without realizing that there are, indeed, gay and lesbian students enrolled, gay and lesbian parents visiting on parents' weekend, although I don't suppose I had given it much thought when Stephen was in residence.

But as I looked around Woodberry Forest at all those lovely southern women who didn't wilt in the heat, all those southern fathers filled with that unique, slyly self-deprecating southern humor, I knew it was impossible that any of these middle-class southern parents had a gay child. It was inconceivable; it wouldn't be permissible. I was convinced that not one of those families would ever face the complicated diplomacy that my own family might have to navigate in order to adhere.

I wanted to get out of there, but I was sad not to be comfortable anymore in this society. These people all around me chatting to each other, calling greetings and good-byes back and forth, snapping pictures of each other, seemed to me to have not only a sense of entitlement, but a smug sense of . . . *place*. A place in the world, an identifiable and enviable place in the social strata. And, more offensive to me than anything was what seemed to me to be an implicit agreement to conform to standards or habits that would maintain everyone's comfort. It was no doubt an unfair characterization, but I didn't think that any of these people would ever rock the boat. I sensed an insistence on a sameness of conduct and attitude that could never again include me or my family.

I was sinking rapidly into a maudlin state of mind until I caught sight of Jack and Stephen coming across the lawn together, obviously glad to be in each other's company, excited about their trip, heads leaning toward each other as they walked, involved in a conversation that had an exclusively fraternal quality of its own. I felt a thrill of adrenaline when I saw them, and before they saw me. I was grounded by the sight of them—I *knew* them! Here they were—the center of this kaleidoscope of activity and people. They seemed extraordinary to me in their beauty, their wit, their intelligence. The lovely grounds of Woodberry Forest School stretched away behind them, and they were golden, golden boys as they threaded their way through the crowds, oblivious of their surroundings, and laughing, filled with pleasure. Although I always think it's a rather odd phrase—often indicating a sort of proprietary credit—I was overcome with pride at being the parent of these two young men.

When Charles and I dropped the boys off at Stephen's friend Natalie's house in Washington, D.C., where he and Jack would join her and one of her friends, who were also going to the institute in Oaxaca, we had very little time for good-byes. In less than fifteen minutes we were on the road again. We were both weary and

didn't say much of any importance to each other except
to agree that we would stop for the night at a motel about
six o'clock.

I don't remember where we stopped that evening,
but it was at a motel that had no restaurant, and the desk
clerk directed us to an Italian restaurant whose virtues he
extolled, although he said it was slightly formal—coat and
tie. We simply remained in the now bedraggled clothes
we had worn to graduation, stopping off at the room to
leave our bags and Jack's computer.

I washed my face with cool water and attempted to
brush my hair, standing at the mirror at the interior end
of the long narrow room. I could see Charles's reflection
as he stood at the other end of the room looking out the
window while he waited for me. He turned and met my
eye in the mirror. "I wouldn't trade our two kids for any
others in the world," he said, with soft-voiced but determined conviction.

I recognized the expression on his face. It was the
look he has when he disagrees with someone but knows
that an argument will be to no avail, that he will never
change the other person's mind. I didn't know with
whom he had been debating in his head, but I realized he
had had the same feeling of disjointedness that I had
among the throng of parents and friends at graduation.
And I realized, too, that he had experienced an epiphany
similar to the one that had overwhelmed me as I had
watched my sons come toward me across the beautifully
groomed grounds of the school.

We didn't even discuss any of this during dinner; we
had used up our emotional energy in the four days we

had spent in Virginia. And the restaurant recommended to us turned out to be a neighborhood gathering place, full to the brim, and in which we were regarded with tactful suspicion. Our feeling of disconnectedness was only enhanced, although we didn't talk about that either. Neither of us slept well that night, and we got on the road early.

As we drove through Pennsylvania and New York State, the trip didn't seem to me to be getting shorter; the remaining miles seemed endless. I was anxious to be at home again, where we would know exactly where we were, where familiarity would be such a comfort. We pulled into a rest stop to eat sandwiches and apples we had picked up at a convenience store before getting on the interstate, and I found some national news on the radio, which we listened to in silence. At the end of the broadcast, when no plane crash had been reported anywhere in the world, I relaxed and finished my apple. Jack and Stephen's flight had landed safely in Mexico City. "Well, that's good," I said to Charles, only half kidding. "The opals I borrowed worked as well as my earrings after all."

We sat for a while in the warm breeze, and we began to reminisce about our house as if we had been away for years. We talked about sitting on the porch and listening to music in the evenings, about each dog and cat individually, explaining to one another why we were so fond of each one. We sat there quickly eating lunch so we could hurry and get home once again.

That evening when we pulled into our driveway, the dogs were as ecstatic and foolish in their delight at seeing us as we had counted on their being. They stood with their paws up on the fence and sang to us enthusiastically, and our cats wound around our legs as we brought our things in from the car. Our big, sweet, dim-witted tabby was purring and happy to have us at home again, but his smaller brother was verbal in chastising us for having been away.

We gave the animals fresh water and petted them. We went through the house and opened the windows to let some fresh air into the musty rooms. We turned off lights and opened curtains, expecting at any moment to be overtaken by that incomparable feeling of returning to the place where you know you belong. But finally I ended up sitting out on the porch with Charles, looking off into the meadow where a herd of deer was grazing, and still feeling edgy—feeling oddly dispossessed. We had arrived at our house, and I had been yearning for the relief of recovering from homesickness, but it eluded me.

It wasn't the lost camaraderie of southerners that had made me ill at ease at Woodberry, among the families of graduating seniors. It had nothing to do with anyone else at all. Charles and I had retreated from the possible comfort of a community and sought sanctuary within our own rooms. I had come into my house expecting to feel comfortable among my belongings, my dogs and cats, the familiar play of light from morning to night as it moved across the yard, the views from every window—predictable but changing with the weather and each season. But our house had taken on the dimensions of a single closet, and a closet is no place like home.

Chapter Five

Caring
for
Children

THE OPAL EARRINGS TURNED UP a few days after we were back in Williamstown. I came upon them by accident in one of my desk drawers where they were mixed inexplicably with paper clips I keep in a blue plastic box. Perhaps I had taken them off to talk on the phone. I wore them every day of that summer and for a long time after that. I still put them on now and then under certain circumstances, but they are, after all, only a pair of opal earrings.

When we returned from Jack's graduation, we discovered that Charles's mother was not at all well. He began making immediate arrangements to leave for Georgia. And there was a terse message on the answering machine from my friend Charlotte in Maryland. Her son,

Scottie, who is my honorary godson, had been hospital-
ized. Would I please call?

Before we left for Jack's graduation I had mailed off
a card, a silly, token gift, and a nonfrivolous check to mark
Scottie's graduation. I didn't know then that he had not
graduated from the independent school near Washington
he attended as a day student. When I heard her message
on the machine, I realized that I hadn't spoken to Charlotte for over two months, whereas we had usually
touched base at least once a week. I had met Charlotte
eighteen years earlier in a gynecologist's office, in Columbia, Missouri, before her first child and my second were
born.

She had struck up a conversation with Stephen, who
was restless in the waiting room. She offered to watch him
while I saw my doctor, and they had become instant
friends, even though Stephen was not yet two years old.
Stephen and I stayed on in the waiting room until Charlotte was called by the receptionist for her appointment.
We were both nearly five months pregnant, and it's true
that simultaneous pregnancy is nearly a guarantee of temporary friendship, and that Charlotte and I did talk about
being pregnant. But that first afternoon we also talked
about having relocated to Missouri from our native re-
gions—she from the D.C. area, I from the deep South.
We talked about the books we read, the movies we had
seen. Over the next weeks our checkups continued to
coincide, and we were enrolled in the same Lamaze class.

We became friends far past discussing books and
movies we liked. We discussed Stephen and how he grew,
because Charlotte really wanted to know about *him* in

particular—not about him as a generic baby, so that she might know what to expect when her own child was born. In fact, in the way that adults think of friends, Charlotte was Stephen's first; their lifelong alliance was formed when he was twenty months old. She was the first person outside his immediate family to provide him with a little leeway—even if he was not on his best behavior, he had her long-term, unconditional approval.

Charlotte is a woman of extremes; she is passionate in her hatreds and affections and even in her appearance. She inhabits few gray areas. She would emerge from her tiny red Karmann Ghia in a motion of unfolding herself, because she is so tall and lanky, and not really beautiful or even conventionally pretty, but impossible not to watch. In the sun, her hair is an unusually deep, glossy red, except for the cloud of tendrils that escape the order she has imposed with a ribbon or a rubber band, and which fly free in a pink haze around her head. She even moves extravagantly, with loose-limbed ease, and she has an equally broad, generous, and explosive humor.

When Charlotte and I were pregnant, Stephen and I often met her for lunch at a little restaurant near campus, and I remember one instance in particular when something struck Charlotte so forcefully with hilarity that she was helpless against her own laughter, so that people began to turn and stare at her. Finally she put her head down on the table, flinging her napkin over her head in embarrassment, and Stephen followed suit.

Whenever she came by for coffee, we settled in the living room where I could keep an eye on Stephen, and we talked about everything. If intention were the barometer, Charlotte and I would be the best parents in the world. We traded books and articles on childcare: Dr. Spock, Dr. Salk. And it was Charlotte who introduced me to the luminous book by Dr. T. Berry Brazelton, *Infants and Mothers*. We discussed and dissected and pondered the information in these books with passion generally reserved for great fiction, and perhaps that was appropriate.

We also discussed our marriages, and some of the details of hers worried me, although I didn't tell her so outright. We talked about our siblings—she had four—and our parents, the Vietnam War, the death penalty, the president, the women's movement. I talked to her about my writing, which was unpublished then, and about which I was generally silent, because the need and desire to succeed at it made me uncomfortably vulnerable. She told me how hard she was working for her doctorate and wondered whether she could keep up the pace once she had a child.

Charlotte was the friend of my twenties. I am embarrassed sometimes that much of what I confided to her then seemed to me to be uncanny bits of wisdom born of my singular experience of life. Over the years I've discovered that my experience was neither extraordinary nor even particularly unusual, but she met me at a time when I was brimming over with the news of everything I had found out in my first twenty-odd years. Charlotte is not particularly reflective, but I suppose that if she ever remembers that time of our lives, she may feel equally chagrined.

It seems to me, though, that I blithely revealed to

Charlotte much of the pettiness of my character. I told her one day in passing that I was hurt in a mild way that Stephen's godmother had not returned the compliment and asked me to be a godparent to either of her children.

"But you aren't Catholic."

"It shouldn't matter. She knows the things I believe." It's uncomfortable to remember that I was ever that petulant. Charlotte is Catholic, also, but when her son, Scottie, was born, she asked me to be his godmother. At least I summoned the grace to decline to be anything but an *honorary* godmother, because when I considered the real role a godmother should play, I knew I couldn't fulfill the obligation.

Eventually—as soon as we had become attached to the town and the area—we both moved away from Columbia, she only a year after Charles and I had relocated to Williamstown. When she and her husband were divorced, Charlotte moved with her three children to Maryland, near her hometown of Washington, D.C. But we've stayed in close touch.

And that spring of 1991, when we returned from Jack's graduation, I found out that twice in the last weeks of the semester Scottie had come to school late and presumably drunk. His advisor had sent him to the infirmary used by the residential boarding students, where he recovered before going home. The school had defied its own rules by failing to inform Charlotte. The third time he was sent to the infirmary he slit his wrists, and without Charlotte's knowledge or permission, the school had him transferred to the psychiatric unit of a private hospital. The first Charlotte heard of any of this was when the hospital located her at her office to obtain permission to admit him.

She arrived at the hospital simultaneously with his advisor, who was there to tell Scottie that the school no longer considered him an enrolled student, because the administration had word that he had been using drugs. Scottie was not to come on campus, but his family would be allowed to come to the school on the following Saturday to collect his things. This man—a teacher who presumably had acted as Scottie's confidant and protector—stood in that hospital room with Charlotte and said all this to Scottie, who was physically restrained and nearly comatose, and was probably unable to understand or maybe even to hear. But Charlotte had heard everything Scottie's advisor said with what must have been a terrible clarity, and I realize now that she went into a state of shock herself.

The summer before his and Jack's senior year, Scottie and a friend had stayed with us overnight before continuing on the second leg of their hike over the Appalachian Trail. That was the first time I'd seen him in almost five years, but we'd had a good time with him and his friend Rebecca. Scottie had become "Scott," of course, and he was charming and witty. I was struck by how much he looked like his father, although his hair had remained the color of his mother's. He had seemed cheerful, healthy, good-looking—a successful teenager. I had been heartened and reassured by his visit.

When he and Jack were five years old, Scottie had

stayed with us for five days, and I had never told Charlotte what a disaster it had been. He was a deeply angry child, and she must have been aware of it. His parents had just settled their divorce, and the two younger children, one just an infant, were staying with Charlotte's mother. We had all thought it would be nice for Scottie to visit us in Williamstown while Charlotte waited in Maryland for the movers to deliver her furniture, the arrival of which had been hard to schedule since it was being delivered as a partial shipment after several others had been off-loaded at other destinations. She was uneasy about moving Scottie into a new situation before she had a chance to wrench a little order into her life, and we were hoping to help make her relocation a bit easier.

But Scottie had never been to Williamstown, was unfamiliar with our house, and scarcely remembered us, although Charlotte stayed for two days before driving on to Maryland to intercept the movers. That visit was an ill-conceived idea all around, and I put Scottie's anger down to the recent turbulence of his life, although in Scottie's case, for reasons that I think were based more on instinct than substance, I suspected even then that that explanation was too simplistic. Scottie had been angry for a long time, and there was an unusually closed off quality about his rage—it seemed only to be about himself. After the first few days of terrible clashes with Jack and Stephen, I realized we should leave him alone, as much as that was possible, and as long as he was busy and safe. Scottie resented me, and it's hard to maintain genuine affection for a determined child who is not your own and who dislikes you, and no doubt I had begun to sound false in whatever kindnesses I extended to him. He grew increasingly hostile as the days went by.

One afternoon when I thought I had sorted the children out into separate and peaceful activities, I sat down in the living room away from them all to try to finish a paragraph I had been working on for several days. My concentration when I am at work is emotionally fragile but, in a practical way, pretty fierce. When my children were young I could block out all but emergency sounds, and I didn't pay much attention to Scottie when he came quietly into the room; I don't know if he asked me some question that I failed to answer. I knew he had sidled up behind my chair, but I was scribbling frantically to get down a thought that I knew would escape if I didn't pin it to the page. Suddenly, though, he managed to overturn a six-foot free-standing bookcase, which crashed down over my head and shoulders. Its force was broken by the high back of my chair, but books fell hard and widely. By the time I extricated myself, I realized that I was not injured but was really hurt, and would be badly bruised.

It has been rare in my life that the people who dislike me manifest their contempt physically; I've generally had to cope only with surprise verbal or written attacks. But Scottie was five years old; he didn't name his fury—he acted on it. And the thing about being the parent of small children is that you are too often tired and enmeshed in the logic of the playground to behave wisely. At first I was simply mad about what Scottie had done, without any other complicated reaction, as though I were only five years old myself. I came up hard against that frail barrier of civilized behavior that exists to prevent adults from striking out at children.

I should have done more, though, than *not* hit him or rage at him. I was so angry that I didn't care that Scottie was just a child, and I could scarcely speak to him at all the rest of the day except in tight-lipped monosyllables. As the day wore on, my face became swollen and bruised on one side where I had turned and a book had struck me; I had a black eye, and my shoulders were sore and stiff from having absorbed the impact of all those heavy falling volumes. I took it personally. I was humiliated, and my feelings were hurt. But I should have alerted Charlotte and tried to make sure Scottie got some help to sort out a fury so large and destructive. I never even told his mother exactly what had happened, because I managed to convince myself that it must have been an accident, although in retrospect I know it was partly misdirected but pure and reasonable rage.

I still have a persistent image from the time of his early visit that exemplifies my notion of Scottie as a little boy. The day after the incident of the bookcase, I came upon him standing alone in front of the kitchen sink, his fists clenched at his sides, and his whole body rigid because he was thirsty and would need an adult to reach the water faucet for him. I took a glass from the cabinet and then turned and reached out my hand and ran it over his head, caressing his beautiful, curly auburn hair—as though I meant to soothe or console him. It was such a seemingly small thing—I had often hugged him or held him on my lap—but both of us knew that this time my gesture was absolutely spontaneous and genuine. I think, now, that it was an involuntary admission of and an apology for my insincerity toward him otherwise. He turned to glance up at me while my hand rested briefly on his head, and we exchanged a wary glance. Just for a moment he slipped beyond his enraged isolation, and what has remained with me for so many years was his expression of resigned hopelessness.

Eventually, during that early visit, his actions seemed to me to verge on being dangerous to himself, my own children, and even our pets. After consulting Charlotte—telling her little more of the truth than that Scottie was unhappy—Charles and I drove him to Maryland to stay with her in her bare-bones and box-filled apartment. I was relieved, but I also felt as though I had let him down inexcusably. I never shirk my role as his honorary god-mother, though. I love to shop for Scottie's birthday. I love to send him presents and cards on holidays or for no reason at all. For the most part, atonement is sinfully rewarding.

When we returned from Virginia, though, that June of 1991, we were alarmed by the report of my mother-in-law's ill health, and Charles had to leave for Atlanta before I had a chance to have other than an informational conversation with Charlotte. The details unfolded in sub-sequent calls—first to Charlotte's answering machine, and then in desperation to Elaine Dressel—a close friend of Charlotte's in Maryland, and a woman I had met and liked. I don't sleep well when Charles is away, and par-ticularly when he made that trip to Atlanta, because I was

worried about his mother and, increasingly, about Charlotte. I was brooding through the nights.

Charlotte is an extension of the family we've chosen,
and whatever was going on in her life seemed to me to
be my business. Elaine told me that since agreeing to have
him admitted to the hospital, Charlotte had only been
allowed to see Scottie twice. He had run away from the
institution after her first visit, and he had made another
apparent attempt at suicide after her second.

"I don't know what I can do," Elaine said to me
over the phone.

"But I don't understand, Elaine. I don't understand
why Charlotte can't see Scottie." The idea of this en-
forced separation infuriated me, made me suspicious of the
hospital where Scottie was being treated. I realized too
late that my voice sounded accusatory, as though it were
Elaine's fault.

She became defensive; she was as anxious and as put
on edge by this as I was. "Well, I don't understand *any* of
this," she said. "Scott really never *did* drink. He never
took drugs! It doesn't make any sense to me."

She was right about Scottie; the last time we had
seen him, he had declined even a glass of wine at my
house and had prepared a meal for us all, because he had
become a vegetarian but had been wise enough even at
age seventeen to understand that it was unfair to impose
his own restrictions on his hostess. He and his friend
Rebecca had arrived at our house with their camping gear
and a bag of groceries and had made vegetable lasagna for
everyone.

"But why would the hospital refuse to let Charlotte even *see* Scottie?" I asked.

"Oh . . . well . . . I think Charlotte would be upset if I talked about it. I think she wants to keep the whole situation as private as possible. She hasn't even told her mother very much. Please don't discuss it with anyone."

I was indignant at the implication and what seemed to me Elaine's proprietary reticence. "Who would I tell? I don't even know anyone else who *knows* Charlotte. Of course I wouldn't discuss her private life with anyone but Charles. If you think I shouldn't even tell Charles, then don't tell me, either. I'll talk to Charlotte in a few days. When she's feeling steadier."

"But Richard might get in touch with you, and it could be even worse for everyone if he finds out about all this. I mean, of course he's going to have to know. For one thing, it's his insurance that will have to cover any prolonged treatment. But right now Charlotte can't even find out exactly what's going on. It would be awful if he got involved right now. He's in Australia on vacation, thank God. He and his wife are traveling, and no one *can* get in touch with him."

This was a chilling idea. Richard is Charlotte's ex-husband, a man who makes me uneasy and whom Charles actively dislikes, which is unusual. Charles generally doesn't bother disliking people; he just puts them out of his mind and avoids them, but anytime Richard's name has come up over the years Charles has become irritable and grudging. Charlotte and Richard had a nasty battle over child support and visitation rights. He is a man who is always reluctant to give up power or what he perceives as an advantage, and he is incapable of loving his own children. He is the only person I have ever met who I really believe is an egoist, and I might pity him if the manifestation of his personality were not so harmful to people I love.

I was chastened, and Elaine finally continued. "Charlotte was in bad shape when she told me what had happened. I may not have it all straight. From what I could gather, Scott's doctors are afraid he might hurt Charlotte if she came to visit again. And I guess Scott is afraid, too. Afraid he might hurt Charlotte, I mean."

"You mean hurt her feelings?"

"They're afraid he might attack her," she said.

"Elaine! That's ridiculous! Why would they even *tell* her that? No wonder she sounds so stunned! That must have nearly devastated her!"

Elaine was weary; I could hear it over the phone. "What she told me was confused, and I didn't want to make it worse by asking questions. Scott told his doctors that he made some sort of promise to his mother when he was a child. Some promise that he knows he can't keep." She paused, and there was silence on the line between us while I waited for her to explain. Her voice was reluctant, touching gingerly over the melodrama of her message as though she were sounding out the notes of a new piece of music on the piano for the first time. "He says that unless *she* dies, *he* will have to die, because he can't keep the promise."

I was horrified; I hadn't understood that the situation was not only deeply alarming but ongoing. "My God! What did he promise?" I thought of Charlotte and her children and revised the question. "What does he think he promised?"

But Elaine said that Charlotte had no idea what he might be thinking. She was afraid Scott was delusional. She was terrified that he might have moved into the terrain of some kind of unknowable mental disorder, and the doctors wouldn't answer her questions. In fact, Scottie's doctors had missed two appointments they themselves had set up with Charlotte. I continued to try to reach her but had to be satisfied with leaving messages on her machine, and she didn't return my calls.

For several days I wandered around the house unable to settle long at anything. I vacillated between anger and sorrow and puzzlement on behalf of Charlotte and Scottie. I worried about his sisters, Anna and Katherine, and wondered why no one ever answered Charlotte's phone. With Charles away, I had no one at all to talk to, because I wasn't at liberty to discuss Charlotte's life even with people who didn't know her personally, and I wasn't at liberty to discuss my own life because it seemed to me that it would be a betrayal of Stephen, and of Jack, too.

I told Charles only a little bit about what had happened to Charlotte and Scottie when I spoke to him on the phone. I could tell from the way Charles talked about his mother that he had a feeling that this was the last good visit he would ever have with her, although he didn't say so. His family is unusually reticent about bad news, and a kind of nostalgia crept into his voice when he related various conversations he and his mother had each day. I was fighting deep sorrow, and I began to feel trapped and overwhelmed by all the elements of my life about which I needed to keep silent.

When I finally did reach Charlotte once again she was calmer, and I thought that she sounded bitter, which seemed to me to be a strange reaction from Charlotte, of all people.

"I can't believe Scott did this just before graduation," she said. And this struck me as such an odd response that I didn't even address it.

"How is Scottie? When is he coming home?"

"Well, they're going to discharge him in three weeks because his coverage runs out by then, and I can't get in touch with Richard." She didn't seem to me to have a grip on what this might mean for Scottie, and I was taken aback once again.

"But should he come home then, Charlotte? What does he say?"

"He can't come here," she said, not really answering any question I had asked, but filling me with dread, because it was as if she were making an effort not to have to consider Scottie at all.

"Do you know," she went on, "that he was going to get the Drayton Award for Lacrosse. The Science Prize, and the Harvard Book Prize. I just can't believe that he would do this and ruin everything like this. He was taking six courses. Four of them were advanced placement, and until this semester he had the highest academic average of anyone who ever attended the school!" It hadn't been my imagination when I thought she sounded bitter; it was clear in her voice and was shocking to me.

"But, Charlotte! How is Scottie? What *happened* to him?"

"He's not even allowed to go back to campus. Anna and Katherine are going over to get his stuff from his locker. And his lacrosse gear. They're going on Saturday. I have to work Saturday because I've gotten so far behind. I've missed so much time." Her voice was busy as she spoke, with a kind of buzzing indignation. "And the school says it has to notify Stanford. They may rescind his acceptance now. Now that this happened."

"How can they do that? They've already accepted him?"

"His advisor said that his acceptance was on the condition that he satisfactorily completed high school. Anna thinks that Scott actually could have graduated mid-semester. He may have enough courses. But the school won't recommend acceptance now. When this happened the third time, Scott smashed the window of the school infirmary."

I was at a loss for a response, because Charlotte seemed unreachable in her furious and peculiar indignation. She was brittle to the point of breaking. I understand now that she was afraid, but I was quietly angry at her then, for refusing to answer me or even to think about what I was asking. Later Elaine defended her by reminding me what an enormous financial sacrifice Charlotte had made to send her children to private schools in the face of Richard's outright scorn for the idea.

"But what's wrong with Scottie?" I asked her. "Or is he all right? What is he going to do?"

Elaine didn't know, and I was feeling so oppressed

by the sad news that I finally had to get out of my house and at least be in the presence of other people. I decided I would be safe from chance encounters with good friends at the Clark Art Institute, because it's avoided by local residents during the summer. They prefer to visit in the off-season when the museum is nearly empty.

I know the paintings so well that I just wandered aimlessly, basking in the passive company of the tourists who worked their way carefully through the rooms. I was haunted by Scottie's sad and dangerous sense of honor. What kind of promise could be so binding that, if it couldn't be kept, made Scottie believe he couldn't allow himself to live, didn't believe he could *remain*—not just in his mother's vicinity—but anywhere on earth?

I sat down on a bench for a while to watch a student who had set up her easel and a camp stool and was making a study of a Monet. The museum was comforting because it was busy with people who required nothing of me, who knew nothing about me, and about whom I knew nothing at all except that I was glad to wander among them.

The whole building cheered me just as when I was growing up in Baton Rouge and was taken on a field trip to the state capitol. The atmosphere of that rather grand, official, civic building always brought on in me a mild state of euphoria. I loved the sounds of my footsteps on the marble floors, the muted hush of possibly urgent conversations among small clusters of men in business suits, the idea of my own self somehow connected to a larger, more significant world. And museums affect me much the same way. At the Clark, everyone around me spoke softly, as people do in museums. The guards wandering the halls were a quiet, oddly reassuring presence. I was soothed.

Even when I bumped into Sandra Wexworth I felt enormous goodwill toward her, although I had hoped to avoid seeing anyone I knew. But Sandra was something of an exception, anyway. I didn't know her very well; she wouldn't expect to discuss anything particularly personal about either of us, and I knew she had just come back from having spent a year in Italy. I was curious to find out how she had liked it.

I suggested we sit down for a moment in a room sparsely visited by tourists, since it is primarily devoted to antique furniture and silver, with only a few fairly obscure paintings on the walls. I was overcome all at once by a buoyant expansiveness after the days of keeping to myself, of brooding and grieving.

"Rome must have been fascinating," I said. "It must seem strange to be back in Williamstown. You probably should have come back and spent a month in New York. To decompress. To reduce the culture shock. Being back in the Berkshires must be strange." I was straining for a light tone.

"All of Italy was amazing. It was an adventure. I loved most of it, but a year is a long time. I really got quite homesick, and that surprised me. I grew up in Los Angeles. I didn't know I liked Williamstown that much," she said. Her smile was slightly rueful, indicating that the whole experience was a long story, and we weren't close enough friends that she wanted to tell it or that I wanted to hear it. Her answer forestalled any further questions.

She leaned toward me and put her hand on my

forearm. "But, Robb, you may not have heard that I've finally started my own business? I've branched out on my own."

"Oh, no, I didn't know that. That's terrific. What are you doing?"

"Well, I'm doing something I would never have dared try before. It's a branch of real estate, really. But I'm trying to fill a vacuum in Berkshire County. Of course I *will* handle sales if it works out that way. For instance, if there's a lease with an option to buy. But I'm concentrating mostly on handling rentals for the theater and the college. Primarily short-term, but yearly rentals, too."

"That's great," I said. I didn't really have an opinion about Sandra opening her own business, but I didn't want to be rude. "What made you decide to take a step like that?"

Her hands fluttered upward to suggest the inexplicability of it, and then she settled her hand on my arm once again. "Sometimes you just have to take a leap," she said. "Mark really loved Italy. He traveled a lot. I had plenty of time to do some real thinking. I had a chance to get my priorities straight. His company's talking about relocating him there for the next three years. At least three years. He's still in Milan, in fact. I'm not sure I'm willing to do that, though, and it seemed like a good idea to try out some possibilities of my own. The children are pretty much settled in their own lives, but they're all three within striking distance of the Berkshires."

Sandra is an attractive woman, impeccably groomed by New England standards, with a rather clipped manner, and I had always assumed that everything about her life ran like clockwork. An odd memory popped into my head of Jack in the fourth grade, studying for a weekly test and going over and over a spelling trick: "When you *assume* you make an 'ass' of 'u' and 'me.'" And I smiled involuntarily and probably unkindly.

"We had an awful time when we relocated for Charles's sabbatical," I said, to cover my smile and also with some idea of encouraging her. "We thought we'd found really great renters for our house, and we rented it for next to nothing so they would take care of our pets. But they ended up subletting the other rooms of our house to *three* more people! The house was a wreck when we got back! At least they took good care of the animals. But it was a terrible experience. It would have been great to have had someone in town handling it, Sandra. I think this'll be great. I think you'll have a real success with this."

She grimaced slightly. "Well, I haven't been able to prevent every terrible experience, I'm afraid," she said. "I'm here to meet James Purcell about a rental I handled for him."

James Purcell has an office at the Clark, and I realized that I had detained Sandra on her way to meet him. I stood up, and so did she, still lightly grasping my arm. "I shouldn't have kept you," I said. "I thought you were just browsing like I was. But it's really nice to see you again!"

But she wasn't in a hurry to move away. She leaned her head closer to mine as a small group of museumgoers slowly moved among the collection of silver. "Oh, well, I don't know how I'm going to handle this. I arranged a theater rental. Two young men took Jim's house for the semester he was in Fort Worth." Her tone was intimate and confidential. "But you wouldn't believe what they did. They painted the bathroom *completely* black! Jim is furious. They're *gay,* of course." She looked at me slyly and then her expression became impassive when I didn't react. "The men I rented to, I mean." But I still had nothing to say. "Well, I don't know *why* I told you that. I knew they were in the theater. They're both very dramatic. One of them dresses in nothing *but* black. But it never occurred to me to put into the lease that they shouldn't paint the rooms! There's a general clause that might help, but the damage deposit isn't going to cover it."

A few times in my life I have been unable to speak— literally. My lips freeze shut with a sensation similar to that of finding that your arm or leg has gone numb. The muscles of my face become rigid and tingly, and I cannot open my mouth. It happened to me then. I could feel adrenaline surging through my body; I could feel my heart racing, but I don't remember registering any emotion while I stood there unresponsive. I must have looked alarming to her, though, in some way, because she made her excuses and went off without my having said a word, and I turned around and made my way out of the building.

Sandra is not a hateful woman, or, at least, I had never thought of her as someone filled with hate. And what she had expressed was hard to pin down. It was some sort of disdain, although not unusually vicious—fairly mild, in fact, when measured on the spectrum of American intolerance and hatred of gays. But my reaction to it was severe.

That awful sensation of paralysis didn't go away as I reached the car, and, in fact, it spread to my arms and legs, which became so stiff that I was afraid to try to drive. I sat in the front seat for a little while, waiting for this odd attack to pass, leaning my head back against the headrest in an emotional daze, looking out at Stone Hill, which rises behind the museum serenely, with cows grazing on its flanks.

There have been various but infrequent occasions in my life when imagination, sensation, and event—no matter how trivial—have become enmeshed, so that they take on the aspect of heightened reality. My first remembrance of this sort is of a time when I was four years old and was supposed to be taking a nap. Everything in my being tells me that I took flight, in that Nashville afternoon, skimming the ceiling of the bedroom of the house my parents rented while my father finished his residency at Vanderbilt. It cannot be true, but I find it nearly impossible to *dis*believe, because I recall it intellectually and also in every muscle and fiber, in the pit of my stomach.

Otherwise, until that day in the parking lot of the museum, these peculiar states have been less dramatic. For instance, when I was in the seventh grade, some friends and I were in my backyard one afternoon listening to the after-school request hour on the radio, and I was dancing with someone when suddenly my feet did not touch the ground as I moved. I am a good dancer, but for a small slice of time I was extraordinary, the best dancer in the world. I remember it exactly; I know it is so, and I know it is not so.

Three times I have experienced déjà vu, which isn't

quite the same, but which occurs with equal vividness of sensation. And once I have seen an animal that I couldn't have seen, and now it is twice that I have seen people for a scant second who could not have been there. Those impossible visions are so ordinary when they occur that it is a sensation I have made use of several times in my fiction, because the experience has always intrigued me, and I suspect it occurs with fair frequency in many people's lives.

The animal was a long-dead Siamese cat from my childhood. I saw him sitting on the couch of my first apartment in New Orleans one day as I entered the room. I thought nothing of it as I registered his being there, turned to put down my purse, and then swung back in alarm to find, of course, that he was not there. But I looked all around the room before I remembered that he was dead. And once, when I was about twenty, I was moving through the line at a Picadilly Cafeteria in Baton Rouge when I turned to my right, slightly, and saw Felice Bordelon standing next to me, looking exactly as she had when I had seen her last in the third grade, with long braids, which I envied, all the way down her back. I smiled and turned away to tell the server I wanted a piece of fried chicken, and, naturally, when I startled and looked around, Felice was not there. There is no reason that I can think of for these peculiar reveries; Felice was just someone in my class; I scarcely knew her.

But the last time I experienced anything like this was that afternoon in the parking lot of the Clark Art Institute, when I became aware, out of the corner of my eye, that my young cousin Bobby was sitting in the passenger seat, waiting for us to leave. I didn't see his face, only his leg and tennis shoe and his forearm and hand, which rested on his thigh. It was perfectly natural and expected, though, for a fraction of a second, that he was with me. I can still see the exact angle of his foot as it rested on the floor mat, cocked slantwise at the ankle and resting against the interior divider that encloses the gear shift. I can see his shoelace tied unevenly, the left loop of the bow too long and about to come undone, the frayed ends of the laces. I know he was there, but I know just as surely that he was not, because Bobby hanged himself at age twelve.

I had heard the news about Bobby when I was far away in Missouri and busy being newly married. I had never known him very well, because I was ten years older than he was. He was known for being extremely bright, I think, especially in mathematics—or maybe that was his younger sister. I do remember that he was a strikingly beautiful young boy, but always out of sync with the rest of his family in some way that I no longer remember. I probably wasn't much aware of Bobby at all in the early 1960s. The rest of what I know about him is knowledge I acquired in spite of my teenaged self-absorption as I passed through a room where my mother and grand-mother were talking, or when Bobby and his family visited my grandparents while I was there also.

"Well, with Lawrence away so much, I don't sup-pose it's unusual that Bobby is so much like Janine. He's Janine's child," my grandmother said.

"Do you think he might be . . . um . . . rebelling? With Lawrence gone so much? Maybe he's under too much pressure to be the *man* of the house," my mother said once. And what probably caught my attention was that, although there was no intonation of censure in what they said, there was a faintly plaintive note of concern. I must have caught hold of the fact that something perplexed them. Something was amiss. Something they perceived about Bobby drew forth these peculiar, slightly defensive remarks. And yet their concern was *fond;* I could hear it in their voices, although whatever they were saying otherwise was not very interesting to me at age fifteen or sixteen. I was as close in age to his mother, who was my favorite aunt, as I had been to him, and his life came to an end just as mine had taken a complicated turn.

When my mother called with the terrible news of his death, she said my aunt and uncle had searched the house for a note, for any clue, but they hadn't found anything to explain it. Some classmates had volunteered the information that there had been a popular television show a few days earlier on which someone had demonstrated how to tie all sorts of slip knots. Maybe he had been trying out a trick noose?

There was nothing else Aunt Janine and Uncle Lawrence, and all the rest of the family, could imagine except that Bobby's death was accidental, and it's a possibility I've considered often in the past two years. I've thought a lot about what is and isn't accidental, which is slightly different from what is or isn't purposeful. I am certain, for instance, that Scottie meant to overturn that bookcase so long ago, and try as I might, I simply don't believe Bobby hanged himself by accident. At twenty-two I had been shocked and sad that he had died, but at forty-four, when I turned to find him *not* in the car with

me, I was at last overcome with anger, grief, and a puzzling but overwhelming feeling of responsibility. I could
scarcely breathe by the time I pulled into my garage, and
I was panicky.

I think I instinctively sought shelter at the center of
our house. It's where I would go if there were ever
tornado warnings in the Berkshires. The main staircase of
the original building turns the corner halfway up, and at
that level a second, unmatched and ill-planned flight of
stairs breaks away in the opposite direction to a later
addition. It is the spot our German shepherds choose,
because from that vantage point they can monitor all the
comings and goings of people in our house. And it's
where I sat down, away from all the windows, but with
pale light shifting over the stairs from the front hall.

I sat on a step leading to the long book-lined hall to
the rear bedroom and my study, leaning against the doorframe, embracing myself around the waist in an attempt
to ease a panic-induced nausea. I studied the framed pictures hanging in rising progression up the stairs—repro-
ductions of John White's sixteenth-century watercolors of
animal life on the North American continent.

I studied each print in an effort to calm myself.
Charles's parents had ordered them from the American
Heritage Society and passed them on to us when we were
first married. I had framed them at a shop that charged
only cost if you did the work yourself under their tutelage.
On the upper wall hung old family photographs of
Charles's family and those of my family that I had inher-
ited when my great-uncle died, including a beautiful portrait of my cousin Bobby's father as a boy. I sat on the

stairs above the print of the turtle and another of a flam-
ingo, and beneath the gaze of my grandfather and the
tinted portrait of my beautiful grandmother wearing a
flapper headband.

I have rarely in my life been as disoriented, with
thoughts flying through my head seemingly at random.
And a poem from childhood teased me, a verse that was
meant to be whimsical but that had always unaccountably
alarmed me as a child. I could only get hold of it in bits
and pieces. Eventually, months later, when I described the
sense of it and the fragments I could remember, a friend
found it for me in *The World of Christopher Robin*, and the
poem still seems to me to be not just melancholy, but
ominous.

> Halfway down the stairs
> Is a stair
> Where I sit
> There isn't any
> Other stair
> Quite like
> It.
> I'm not at the bottom
> I'm not at the top;
> So this is the stair
> Where
> I always
> Stop.
>
> Halfway up the stairs
> Isn't up;

And isn't down.
It isn't in the nursery,
It isn't in the town.
And all sorts of funny thoughts
Run round my head:
"It isn't really
Anywhere!
It's somewhere else
Instead!"

I sat still on the stairway, puzzling over that and other nursery rhymes; shreds of incidents of my children's childhoods occurred to me and faded away without apparent significance. I thought about how Charlotte and I survived the several years together through our children's babyhood. The endless reading and discussing of human children that we engaged in, the careful attention we paid to those steady-voiced, well-published experts in child development.

I was in the grip of a dreadful bafflement; I both yearned for some sort of clarity of mind and was terrified to leave behind my hard-won definition of myself as a person who has a firm grasp of human motives and desires. But it was as though enlightenment had been stalking me all day and finally caught up to me on the landing of the stairway, where I had run out of the energy to avoid it. I sat there and was overcome with the absolute certainty of the promise from which Scottie could not extricate himself. I closed my eyes and leaned my forehead on my knees. I covered my ears with my hands, in an effort not to know the truth. I tried to tuck myself away from my own knowledge, because it was too painful and too dangerous to my own peace of mind.

But the idea was there, and I was unable to screen it out. Scottie hadn't promised his mother anything; he had unwittingly accepted the unspoken dictum of society that he must never, ever, reveal an essential part of his being. I suddenly felt absolutely sure that Scottie thought he had promised his mother that he wouldn't be gay. He had begun to absorb a version of "don't ask, don't tell" from his earliest moments of sensibility. To ensure the comfort of all those people who cared for them, Scottie and Stephen, and probably Bobby, not only taught themselves silence, but learned fear. And they had incorporated a deadly sense of shame into the core of their existence. I huddled against the doorframe as the light began to fade.

As the house grew darker, anger began to overtake me, and it was a great relief. I was eager to accommodate anger, because it takes up so much room and it is unambiguous. I got up for a moment to fetch the books that had been our bibles—Charlotte's and mine—finding them exactly where I had put them, probably eight or nine years earlier, after I had last consulted them. I settled again on the stairs with several volumes, all of them worn and used; petrified, mysterious, puréed food still adhered to the cover of a paperback by Dr. Spock. I consulted the index for "Homosexuality" in *Dr. Spock Talks with Mothers*. I found nothing. "Suicide." Not a word. I looked up "Rage": no reference. "Depression," "Despair"—no listing.

I searched through *Baby and Child Care*, again by Dr. Spock, finally looking under "anger," and turned to the reference for "anger in child in adolescence, 419–421." When I flipped to these pages I found a smug little piece that was infuriating in its wrongheadedness. I turned to Dr. Brazelton, whose books I had always counted on for the more subtle interpretations of children's sensibilities. Dr. Brazelton's books deal primarily with infants and young children, but my own son had told me that he first realized that he was somehow "different" at the age of two or three. I researched carefully, but Dr. Brazelton had nothing to offer me.

I was enraged. I cursed those men, yelling out loud right there on my staircase, all alone except for the dogs, who slunk away to the back of the house. I was exhilarated with anger. I tore at the books; I tried to rip them apart, but they were sturdier than they looked, and finally I flung them down the stairs one at a time, and they landed softly with only a whispery, unsatisfactory rustle.

I realized why my extreme, paralyzed reaction was triggered by Sandra Wexworth's disparaging little remark about gays. It brought me face-to-face with the delicately arched eyebrow, the lowered voice, the sly, silky, self-congratulatory innuendo of "us" and "them"—that seemingly inescapable human equation of separation. When I thought of the conspiratory, knowing remarks that I may have been—and probably was—guilty of making myself, I realized that Stephen had been forced into the role of "them" among the four of "us." A minority of one in the whole world as far as he knew. I could scarcely bear it, the knowledge was so painful.

I sat cursing and weeping, feeling as if I were expanding with outrage. How desperately Charlotte and

Charles and I had worked at being good parents! I was breathless with fury and the need for the whole situation to be somebody's fault. We had heeded those steady-voiced doctors in all their complacent assurance, and I am still convinced that despite society's reluctance to confront these issues in the 1970s, those men had always known what I was just beginning to understand.

I believe they had always known about the infinite varieties of sexuality, about the despair children experience when they infer from their surroundings nothing but loathing of what is essential to them. I believe that Dr. Spock and Dr. Brazelton know that a three-year-old cannot choose—in any way that humans understand choice—the elements of his or her own nature. But there had been no one to warn Charlotte of the danger of her assumptions. My Aunt Janine and Uncle Lawrence hadn't been alerted to the risk of the expectations with which they burdened their son. No one had discouraged me and Charles from maintaining the notion that Stephen's life—and Jack's, too—would follow a predictable design, approved of and even lauded by society.

To my mind those people are cowards, those published specialists, as are all the other people who failed us: our pediatricians and the older closeted gays and lesbians who are parents, some of them, and teachers and friends. I don't like or even love them less; they are only, after all, frightened and fallible human beings who generally mean well. But they've lost my admiration. They have made me understand that a lack of bravery—a trait I was previously too foolish to understand or to revere—is also, on some level, a lack of integrity.

Dr. Spock might at least have thrown out a hint early on that our expectations might be hazardous to our children's health. I came upon a picture of him recently, which was taken in 1972 at a Gay Pride parade. He is walking just behind a woman who is holding a hand-lettered sign: PARENTS of Gays UNITE in SUPPORT for our CHILDREN.

I feel sure that Dr. Brazelton knew it; his books shimmer with compassion for and comprehension of the torments of children. I cannot believe a man of his sensitivity and intelligence failed to discern such a significant truth: that parents' assumptions of the heterosexuality of their sons or daughters begin at birth and are a threat to their children's lives.

Thirty percent of all teenage suicides are *directly* attributed to the desperation and eventual hopelessness of gay and lesbian children. I really do believe that Dr. Spock and Dr. Brazelton are writers and doctors who care deeply about the welfare of children, but they didn't say a word. The men whose books we had bought, whose advice we had followed faithfully, were afraid to take the risk of educating us. Those two men alone have illuminated so much about the human condition that I find their irresponsibility shocking; they might have saved lives. But they also would have been disseminating information that their readers would not want to know; they would have dared to strip away the rationale for the last socially acceptable bigotry. And I have found from my own and my family's experience that these authors would have run headlong into a wall of furious opposition. So I do understand their fear in our homophobic society, but no one had the right to let Bobby die when he was twelve years old. No one had the right to let Scottie attempt to die at age seventeen. I believe that these best-selling experts on child behavior know full well the variations of human sexual orientation, and that their silence on the subject is tantamount to neglect and abuse.

For a little while, sitting there on the stairs, I maintained a fine and purifying rage that kept my grief at bay. But finally there was no way to escape the fact that all of us were guilty—Charles and I, and Charlotte, and my aunt and uncle—because this is every parent's business. I was wretched then—and am still—with the burden of my own responsibility for what I believe is an atrocity. We unknowingly let our children grow up in a society that reflects back at them utter scorn for their legitimate emotions. And if our children look to us for confirmation or denial of their dawning understanding of how hard their lives might be, they are met with nothing but a lethal silence, or worse—our unwitting but implied concurrence. So Stephen learned early to live his life in disguise, and Scottie devoted so much of his energy to pretense that by the age of seventeen he had used up all he had, and perhaps Bobby had simply despaired of sustaining a life of such artifice. It's too late to find out.

I can't remember any other time in my life when I have been as sad as I was there alone on the stairs of my house with the light steadily fading. I brooded and agonized over my own failure of imagination and the failure of that of my husband and Charlotte and so many other people. And not only our failure of imagination, but our unforgivable passivity. By doing nothing to stop it, we had countenanced the ongoing injustice of hatred and persecution of gays and lesbians just because we didn't know we were personally involved. We had been too busy or too afraid or too cowardly to take on even a little bit of responsibility for putting a stop to something we knew was wrong. All of us—those published experts, our private doctors and friends—we aren't even bigots. Bigotry is the result of ignorance and inexperience, or it is the reluctance of unintelligent people to respond to any knowledge that contradicts their stereotypes. Bigotry is disheartening; it is loathsome, but it is also blatant. It makes itself known. This was something else altogether.

Sitting there in the center of the house I confronted something I had allowed myself to believe in only tangentially, by observing its shadow, because it is so frightening, and even the act of recognizing it is a full acknowledgment of guilt. It had come right along with the dissipation of my comfortable illusions. It had almost caught up with me in the parking lot of the museum; it had hitched a ride home in the car with me, and it had been inching its way toward me as I indicated surrender by cowering on the stairs. It is a stale-breathed, slothful beast, ancient and exuding a mild stench of sour ease and satisfaction. I was too tired and sad to hold out against its acquaintance any longer, so at last I looked it full in the face and was heartbroken by its awful familiarity. It is the monster of silence and inaction abroad in the world, a permutation of evil. That's what I believed at that moment, and that's what I believe now. I believe that even one voice speaking out, one loud word to deny the enshrouding silence might have prevented Bobby and Scottie from concluding that they couldn't *be* really anywhere, but must be somewhere else instead.

Chapter Six

Losing Heart

WHEN I WAS TEN YEARS OLD I had the idea that when I was grown-up I would find my life. I thought that at age twenty-one I would step into the embrace of an existence that would not be defined, as childhood is, by the desire to get beyond it. And it never occurred to me that my expectation should be other than passive. I assumed that eventual embrace would encompass me in whatever was to be the shape and form and purpose of my continuing presence on the earth, although naturally I thought of it in less coherent terms. It's just that it never crossed my mind to *strive* toward the future; it was more as if I was merely waiting for it to break over me like a wave.

When I was a child no one asked little girls what they wanted to be when they grew up, and, in fact, in the second grade when the boys did projects on careers, our teacher had all the girls do a project on brides. We clipped bridal fashions from magazines, selected the dresses our bridesmaids would wear—even chose our *bridesmaids,* which caused serious distress to any of those seven-year-old girls who had been slow to pick up on the grammar-school politics of popularity. Mrs. Roberts finally decided to have us draw our bridesmaids' names from a box.

I suppose I should be angry about all this in retrospect, but I was half in love with Mrs. Roberts, who was the mother of one of my best friends. Even more to the point, though, is that nothing I ever learned in my sporadic education seemed to apply to me, particularly—I didn't understand that I was supposed to take it personally. The wedding I planned for myself in the second grade was spectacular, and Mrs. Roberts displayed my scrapbook on the "show" table in glorious exclusivity—the only one singled out. I was delighted to have pleased her, but I don't believe I ever connected any part of that project to reality. I never *believed* in it. It was all dresses and hats and shoes and flowers; I never even factored in a groom.

At twenty-one I did get married, but it still didn't seem to me that my life had resolved itself. I decided that it must not be until middle age that life becomes what it is to be. And at last, now that I've reached and passed that milestone, too, I realize that I've misunderstood my own existence for all this time. But, even so, when I think back over 1991, I am struck with an urge to instruct the two people Charles and I were, then, because we surged incautiously into our future.

It seemed crucial to me, for instance, to waste no time alerting Charlotte to what I now knew, because I was certain she would make a leap of imagination and

understand that it was the secret of his homosexuality—
the necessity of keeping his "promise" of heterosexuality—that had triggered Scottie's breakdown.

Charlotte and Stephen had been great admirers of
one another for years. When Stephen visited friends at
Georgetown, he always stayed with or saw Charlotte, and,
in the wake of his visit, she nearly always phoned me in
a state of passionate, quavery-voiced delight and approval.
"Oh, Robb! Stephen's just a perfect person. No, he really
is! He's perfect. He's just *golden,* Robb! He's gorgeous and
wonderful. Completely wonderful. He'll have the whole
world to live in! He can do anything he wants! I really
do love him as if he were my own child." How is it
possible that I didn't realize that another reason I wanted
to confide in Charlotte was that I craved—that I was in
need of—exactly that response?

Charlotte is never mild in her reactions to anything,
but I knew she meant it when she said she loved
Stephen—I know she means it still. And he has always
been enormously fond of her. I *did* believe that if I told
her Stephen was gay, it might make it easier for her
eventually to hear the same thing about her own son.
Scottie had been released from the hospital but still had
not gone home.

The information I got was sketchy, because Charlotte was shocked at the frightening turn her life had
taken, and in some way she was cupping her experience
inward, like a hand of cards, uneasy that anyone else have
a clear view. Scottie had not wanted to go home to her
house, and Charlotte hadn't wanted him to come. He was
spending the summer with Charlotte's mother in Virginia

before he went on to Stanford, which had, indeed, been eager to reissue their invitation to a young man as brilliant as Scottie to enter the incoming class of '93.

Charlotte was frightened, though, because she had no idea what had gone wrong with Scottie and if it was likely to happen again. So it even seemed to me that I *owed* it to Charlotte to tell her that my son had come out to us as a gay man, because, knowing how much she admired Stephen, I thought it might be the least alarming way to introduce my idea about Scottie to her. I thought my telling her about Stephen might open a door between her and her son. But my timing was terrible.

It had been difficult to pin Charlotte down on the phone; she was reluctant to discuss Scottie, almost as if she thought that what had happened to him was somehow shameful. But it is still hard for me to believe that I chose to tell her about Stephen when she was in the hospital recovering from routine, but not minor, surgery. I can't imagine what I could have been thinking except, perhaps, that she would have to hear me out, that she would be a captive audience.

When we were in Virginia for Jack's graduation from Woodberry Forest School, I had overheard a conversation between Stephen and Jack's advisor's wife, Maureen Elgin, that had bothered me ever since. I had been awake all night remembering and brooding about all sorts of things, but particularly about that conversation. Maureen had been describing to Stephen the house they were fashioning for themselves in the countryside near Woodberry Forest School.

"It was an old barn," she said, "completely se-
cluded."

And Stephen had brightened with enthusiasm. "God!
That's my dream. To live like that."

It struck me as quite possible, as I listened to
Maureen and Stephen chatting, that Stephen had grown
so tired of negotiating the difficult path of his existence
in the world that at age nineteen he was longing to retreat.

It is hard enough to learn that it is not the business
of parents to intrude on the ambitions of their children,
whatever they might be. I had tried to remind myself of
that as I remembered Stephen describing to Maureen
Elgin the quiet and isolated life he hoped for. But I was
afraid that when he had summoned the courage to come
out as a gay man, Stephen had assumed he would do so
at the expense of remaining enfranchised in the larger
world. And I was afraid that Charlotte's son had come to
the same conclusion, but that the idea of his own disen-
franchisement was intolerable to him.

Of course, I see now that I had made a huge leap to
reach the conclusion that Scottie was wrestling with coming to terms with homosexuality, although at the time it
seemed to me entirely logical. But I didn't plan to discuss
Scottie in connection with the news I would give Charlotte about Stephen. My idea was that eventually Charlotte would make the connection without my help. Or
perhaps every bit of my instinct was selfish. If there was
anyone on earth I trusted to champion my son it was
Charlotte—against all comers, against all odds. I failed to
realize that I was in no state to handle it if she didn't fly

instantly into advocacy on Stephen's behalf. And I didn't understand that I was counting on Charlotte to dispel the idea of *limitation* that suddenly seemed to me to bracket Stephen's future. Charles was still in Atlanta, and no one else, I thought, would be more unwilling to accept the notion of lessened opportunities for Stephen than Charlotte would be. I was sure of it.

When I finally did get hold of her and told her about Stephen, she was groggy and exhausted and quiet with shock for a few minutes, and then she began to cry. "Oh, my God, Robb. Oh, God. Oh, love, I'm so sad for you. I'm so terribly sorry. Now *nothing* will ever be the same for him. He had *everything* going for him! He would have had a perfect life! Oh, and he would have had the most wonderful children! I'm so sorry, Robb. I'm so terribly sorry! I don't know what to say to help you. I don't know what to say. Now nothing will ever be the same for *any* of you!"

When I hung up I was furious at myself and sick with grief. I had burdened Charlotte with too much responsibility for my happiness at one of the most vulnerable times in her life, and I had also forgotten something crucial, something that I knew quite well. I had been so anxious for Charlotte and Scottie and Stephen and myself that I had chosen not to take into account the astounding complexities of motherhood. Little girls who are never asked what they want to be when they grow up very often end up unconsciously competing with each other through the achievements of their children. I believe now that—inescapably—part of Charlotte's despair about Scottie's breakdown was that she perceived it as a personal defeat. How could she not? And somewhere in her mind had been the inadmissible but bitter idea that it was a defeat I had not suffered as the parent of Stephen and Jack.

She had struggled to provide Scottie with a background that she thought would, by rights, open any door for him, admit him to the highest echelons of society anywhere in the world. Not only did she imagine that she had put the world at his disposal, but, even more important, she believed she had made it safe for him. I think that in spite of herself she believed that he had discarded the mantle of privilege and protection she had painstakingly crafted for him in a spate of peculiarly destructive self-indulgence.

And this conceit and unacknowledged rivalry isn't particular, unfortunately, only to women of my generation. In the way our social order is set up, women—almost upon the moment of giving birth—become competitive on behalf of their children. How soon in relation to the children of their friends do their own children walk, talk, become toilet trained, read? And eventually SAT scores, AP courses, grade point averages, class standings, athletic and academic victories all become part of this subtle but intense competition. Even my younger friends who have just had children are falling into this same pattern—even the innocent pleasure they take in having a "good" baby is an unwitting comparison—and they are setting themselves up for hurt feelings and disappointment when inevitably their own child reaches a difficult stage. Perhaps it is an inescapable trait of maternity. In fact, perhaps it is a way of ensuring infant survival—providing an immediate, vested, personal interest in the welfare of a human child. If any child is going to be a flattering reflection of his or her parent, then it behooves that parent to keep the baby safe and happy and healthy. But if a child deviates in any way from the perceived norm, including the widespread idea that everyone is—or should be—heterosexual, then the parent takes for him or herself a feeling of shame and accountability.

Stephen has always had astonishing social radar, and I can see now with horrified clarity that he absorbed the idea of responsibility for the happiness of his own parents like a sponge. I think that it must have been at a huge cost to himself that he made it so easy for us to be pleased to be his parents. He detected societal competition from the start, from as early, I believe, as two years old, and he became what he thought he needed to be in order to ensure our satisfaction with ourselves as parents. He is, though, who he is; he never compromised his integrity or his character; instead he denied himself freedom of affection, the euphoria of early crushes, the experimentation of early emotional attachments. In our society homosexuals and bisexuals have been so quiet that most people have no idea how many gays and lesbians they know and admire.

Parents of any child need to learn that they must be diligent up to a certain point in helping and taking care of their children. To a certain degree, and for a while, parents must even give over their lives to their children— there is no choice; parenthood is emotionally and physically overwhelming. But eventually parents have to take their lives back and live by and for themselves again. They must relearn a healthy selfishness and simply take pleasure in the continued and occasional company of their children if they are lucky enough to have it.

Because of the peculiar dynamics of motherhood, and the persistent myths of our culture, Charlotte's sorrow on Stephen's and my behalf was genuine, if unwelcome, but it is bound to be true, also, that in her mind it leveled the playing field between us. In ways I hadn't taken into account, she had thought that all the while our children were growing up we were in a contest and—with Scottie's breakdown—that I was winning. My education is spotty, and I never had figured out that *everything* you learn is always personal. Charlotte didn't mean to take some small amount of comfort from what she clearly saw as a tragic circumstance, but along with the pity in her voice I could discern a sort of relief.

It's been several years since that conversation, now, and I've recovered from it slowly, but I don't think Charlotte has, although she's trying. When Stephen was in Washington last year to visit friends, Charlotte and her daughters met him for lunch, and Charlotte didn't call me at all; Stephen did. He was worried, because after Anna and Kat had eaten and gone off to shop, Charlotte had become upset—teary—in the middle of their lunch together. She had suddenly pushed away from the table, with the explanation that she had a meeting she had to get to, and dashed off leaving him stranded at the restaurant with no way to get to the train.

"Something was wrong," Stephen said to me. "She was so strange. Especially after Anna and Kat left. Maybe there were complications with her surgery. Something she doesn't want them to know. I think you should talk to her. I think something's really wrong with Charlotte," he said. "She might have something more wrong with her than she's told you. I felt bad about it. There was no way I could ask her. I didn't think I could without embarrassing her. But it was really strange, Mom. The whole afternoon."

By that time, Stephen was certainly aware that Charlotte knew he had come out as a gay man; he knew Charlotte and I discussed nearly every aspect of our lives over long weekly phone calls. But I hope it didn't occur to him, as it did to me, that her erratic behavior might have anything to do, one way or another, with his sexuality.

"Well, what about you?" I said. "Did you get lunch?"

"Oh, yeah. That didn't matter. It was fine. But I had to hitch a ride to the train. I thought she was going to drive me, but I didn't want to ask her. She was too upset. But I was late and I didn't have any money for a cab."

"Charlotte didn't get you to the train?"

"She asked me if I had a ride, but she was already leaving, and there was something *wrong*—I told her I would be fine. It was just strange, Mom. It was a strange lunch. You should try to find out what's wrong."

But I knew what was wrong with Charlotte, and it's possible that Stephen did too, but he wouldn't have wanted me to be hurt by this closest of friends, especially on his account. I think that afternoon it seemed to her that Stephen was no longer as lucky to be who it turns out he is. She never said so—or, more accurately, she tried *not* to say so. But I think she believed that by being gay Stephen had forfeited what she had considered his glorious possibilities in the world, and she had found it unbearable to be in the company of someone she loved so much, but who had fallen so far through her idea of the social stratosphere.

I could not forgive her self-indulgence for a long time, although I know it was involuntary. I was too angry to call her then, and when I did talk to her again she became teary over the phone. "You must be so proud of Steve and all he's doing," she said. "And no one would ever guess he's gay, Robb. Anna got mad when I asked her that, but she said she would never have known."

I didn't know how to explain to Charlotte how sad it made me to hear her say that, but I also have to remember not to hold my dearest friends to standards I could not have met three years ago. I have to remember that they are trying and eventually will succeed in making the same journey we embarked on. Charlotte said to me a few weeks ago that life has turned out to be such a different enterprise than she expected that she has revised her idea of what it means to exist on the earth. She's beginning to realize that the revelation of a far more interesting and complex world is worth the fearfulness and anguish she went through, but it's an exhausting business, because there is no limit to the endless permutations of homophobia. Every day there is a new assault.

Scottie did come out as a gay man, and he's quite active in the Gay Rights movement at Stanford where he's in his junior year, but he's still on medication for anxiety and now and then suffers incapacitating attacks of

rapid heart beat, chills, and seemingly irrational but alarming fearfulness. I think myself that he has become too
civilized to turn a bookcase over and alleviate his rage; I
also think he's paying a high price for the ability to contain
his anger.

OVER THE PAST FEW YEARS I've finally understood
that I'm never going to come upon the kind of life I
imagined at age ten—a state I envisioned as both tranquil
and static. It really was a surprise to me to discover that
this *living* continues to be a complicated and passionate
and vigorous thing, and even the most serene moment is
played out over an insistent note of urgency, an obbligato
of *progression*. I was born in 1946, but I didn't really figure
all this out until 1991, when we were disturbed on almost
every front; in the purest sense of the word—our com-
placency was interrupted.

When I remember pressing Stephen to tell me if the
man he was involved with was from a "good" family, I
am still astonished and amused. I must have been hoping
that he had happened to be attached to someone from a
family more or less collectively fond of books and kind to
animals. Surely I couldn't have had in mind any sort of
family privileged by birth; I couldn't really have had in
mind some vague notion of an upper-class connection.

Charles and I are both one or two generations away
from Faulkner's Snopes—that is, we aren't from old
money or old aristocratic southern stock. We're Wasps
only because our ancestors immigrated from the British
Isles. As Gail Godwin once said when I was explaining
this to her, "Oh, yes. Pure English. Not *good,* but pure."

And that's it, exactly. The successes of any of our clan—Ransoms, Formans, Dews, and Meeks—have all been self-made, and as far as I know, we aren't related to anyone of particular distinction or celebrity except, perhaps, my grandfather, the poet John Crowe Ransom, and, on Charles's side of the family, the infamous Thomas Dew, and, of course, Aaron Burr—although everyone I knew in Natchez seemed to be related to Aaron Burr one way or another. My cousins and I liked to think he was rather dashing, but I don't know that he's a relation to brag about, anyway.

But now and then our families have produced people who are locally legendary and of remarkable character, none more so than my mother-in-law, Amy Meek Dew. She was the mainstay of her extended family, and she died July 5, 1991. Hers was an expected and reasonable death: she was eighty-five, and her health had rapidly deteriorated in the previous year, but her sudden absence created a vacuum. Her standards of good behavior and propriety were the ones against which every member of her family measured him or herself, because she embodied a quality of kindness combined with certainty. She was reliable in her grace.

Stephen and Jack were anxious to fly to Atlanta for the funeral. We were just as anxious that they not come back from Mexico. We suspected that our Charismatic Christian relations would not be shy about their homophobia, and we hadn't figured out how to handle bigotry if it surfaced—subtly or blatantly—because we were still in the closet ourselves. I am saddened in retrospect by all the years in which I allowed myself to be intimidated by their deep belief in a religion that seems to me to be defined by whom it excludes, defined by "the other." Devotion to the text of an ancient religious document, and the application of its dogma to modern life, strikes me as literally unthoughtful and profoundly offends me.

I am deeply frightened by anyone who believes he or she has the absolute and only answer to the nature of the universe. I am frightened when ideology or religion is used as a rationalization for shunning anyone who doesn't agree or doesn't conform; I am alarmed when any people discover a way to sanctify hatred. I wish the reason for my failure over the years to talk this issue out with my relatives were clearer to me. My reluctance wasn't fair to any of us, because it has held us apart when we might have found a middle ground. We might have found a way to disapprove of the other in the abstract but still forge a close family bond. It isn't as simple as my avoidance of confrontation, although that's part of it. But I've come to think that there is something unusually unsettling about absolute and pious certainty in the face of reason that makes me wary of engaging in any argument or contradiction. I feel a reluctance to point out to anyone that his or her determination to hold on to inflexible beliefs in the face of scientific and social evidence to the contrary is irrational behavior.

My mother-in-law was an observant Episcopalian, never extreme, and, in fact, was distressed by vehemence on any subject, and she was a woman I would have liked to pay homage to. Not only did I admire her; I also loved her. But I was too cowardly to cope with the rest of the family. My other relatives in Atlanta are well-educated, intelligent people, but Charles and I weren't sure we could trust them not to hurt our sons. They didn't know, then, that Stephen was gay, but I knew I wouldn't be able to ignore the disapproval of and hatred in the abstract of one of our own children.

There is an unspoken agreement in Charles's family that confrontation is to be avoided at all costs—not an uncommon conspiracy in the families of alcoholics. Both my father and Charles's were alcoholics, and that may be why it didn't cross my mind to question what, in retrospect, seems to have been a bizarre extreme to have gone to merely to avoid a scene. I didn't go to the funeral, and we insisted that the children stay in Mexico, that it would serve no purpose for them to come home. I don't know how Charles managed to bear up alone under his sorrow over his mother's death and the situation he encountered in Georgia.

Charles had been as sad as I'd ever heard him when I spoke to him the evening after the funeral. He was dispirited beyond exhaustion and sorrow in a way that I couldn't figure out and beyond any comfort I could offer. I didn't want to hang up, because I was worried about him and feeling terrible that I wasn't with him. Finally he said that after the funeral, when people had gathered at the house, one of his relatives had remarked disparagingly to him that the man who wanted to buy his mother's house was gay, and Charles had said nothing more in response than that it didn't matter to him if the man was gay or not.

"I'm just angry," he said. "At myself. I should have said *something*. I should have said it then. There's just so much going on here. I'll tell you about it when I get home."

I had let him get off the phone, because our conversation clearly wasn't making him feel any better.

And his sister-in-law phoned me the next day in a terrible state of agitation. "I can't talk to Charles about anything," Lydia said. "He won't discuss what he wants from the house, and neither will Allen. Can you explain that? I'm going to have the job of sorting through everything in that house, and his mother hasn't thrown anything away in about forty years. Everything's got to be touched. Everything has to be considered. *I* can't talk to Charles. He totally lost it yesterday. He just lost it! He told me all about how he feels about homosexuality! I don't want to go through *that* again!"

I stood there with the phone to my ear stunned, and for a few moments speechless. Finally all I could manage to say to her was that we didn't care about having anything from the house. That Charles's brother was welcome to it all. We didn't want anything, not anything.

But I don't know what Lydia wanted from me. She must have been overwhelmed with the prospect of the enormous chore ahead of her, because I don't think she was concerned about what she and Allen would take from the house. Charles's brother is a warm-hearted, generous-spirited man who lacks greed entirely, as far as I can tell, as does Charles—as, in fact, does Lydia. She is a woman of good intentions, and I hadn't realized that I had been counting on her intelligence to overcome her religious objections to homosexuality. She is someone I had some-

times admired before this incident, but of whom I've had
to be wary. Her goodwill toward me and toward Charles
has been undependable, although she has always been
unfailingly kind to our children.

I had answered the phone in the kitchen, and I was
shaken by having borne the brunt, even for a few minutes,
of her rambling, unfocused distress. But before I could
reach Charles, a succession of calls from various nieces and
the woman who had been my mother-in-law's caretaker
came in, all reporting turmoil about this unprecedented
and heated exchange between Charles and Lydia, which
Charles hadn't mentioned to me. At one point when I
was in a conversation with my niece Polly, she described
in dismay how this had all come about.

"It's such a hard time right now. I just don't know
why everyone got so *mad*. Especially Uncle Charley. I'm
so worried about him. I'm not sure what actually happened," she said. "A lot of people from the church were
at the house after the funeral. I don't know why they were
even talking about gays. I was late getting there. This
woman had been at the funeral for some reason. They
were talking about Grandmother's house. I don't think
she had ever met my grandmother. Anyway, Sharon said
that homosexuals were an abomination in the face of God,
and Uncle Charley just blew up. I didn't know he *ever*
got mad like that!"

When I hung up the phone I was appalled by my
craven silence throughout the various conversations I had
carried on with my relatives during that day. And I
couldn't control the surge of adrenaline that overtook me.
I leaned over the kitchen sink in a paroxysm of dry

retching that was so violent I could scarcely catch my breath, and my eyes watered and burned.

At last when I managed to reach Charles at his mother's house, where he was finally alone, he was so sad that I didn't want to urge him to tell me more than he wanted to talk about. And even now I don't know much more than my niece unwittingly revealed to me, because Charles doesn't like to remember it. He will answer a few questions and then remember something he has to do—a letter to be mailed, a note to be answered, a book he must finish reading for class. And I think I know why it's so painful to him. I believe he's in mourning for the loss of the sustenance he thought he would always be able to draw from his own family.

Charles had to stay in Georgia for several more days, and I ranged around the house in a state of agonized fury. I was bound up in secrets and wanted someone to talk to. I tried to phone my mother and sister, but couldn't reach them. I thought of calling Charlotte but knew that she was in no shape to offer me any advice or comfort. Finally I phoned Beth, the woman who had become the friend of my thirties, and whose discretion is beyond reproach. She has never, as long as I've known her, betrayed a confidence. She does not gossip; she is compassionate and generous, and we had been exchanging the most personal information and concerns for over ten years.

"I don't know what to do to help Charles get through this," I said, after explaining a little of what had happened, but nothing about Stephen, because her children and mine have gone their separate ways, but for a period of years were the closest friends. "I don't know whether to fly down or let it lay."

"Well, Robb, I think you should just let Charles get through it as quickly as possible. Of course, it's terribly unpleasant, but what do you really care, after all, what his family thinks of homosexuals?"

"Oh . . . Beth . . . Steve came out to us a few months ago as a gay man. For the time being that's really just between us, because he and Jack are in Mexico and I don't think he's told Jack yet. But I care very *much* what they think of homosexuals. I would have anyway, but just not so personally. But for Charles this has got to be excruciating."

"Oh, dear, Robb." Her voice was full of sympathetic understanding. "Well, I didn't know, of course. This must be hard. And you both must be so worried about AIDS."

I don't believe there is any time in the lives of parents of gay sons that HIV infection is not a worry somewhere in the back of their minds, and in the minds of their sons as well. It should be in the back of the mind of the parents of any adolescent or adult children; however most people, including me before I knew about Stephen, and including Beth to this day, go about their daily lives in a suspension of *belief*. But this was woefully inadequate comfort that summer afternoon. I couldn't think of how to reply, and I just sat on the stepstool in the kitchen holding the phone without speaking.

Beth waited out the pause for a few moments, and then she said, "A man once said to me . . . a man I admire enormously, and whose judgment I've trusted all my life . . . ," she had lowered her voice as she would to convey very private information, "he once said that homosexuality is something we really can't encourage." She paused again to wait for my reaction, I suppose, but I was just sitting still on the kitchen chair gazing out the glass door at my driveway, where there were two small gray birds bathing in a puddle. I suppose they were sparrows, although I don't know very much about birds. But I think I was trying so hard not to believe that she was saying what she was saying to me that my eye recorded every detail of the birds as they ruffled and fluffed their gray feathers, revealing an unexpected flash of white beneath their outer drab. Even so, they were not very pretty birds. When I made no response, Beth went on. "It's something he said he believed because homosexuality is—When you think about it, Robb, homosexuality is really antifamily. And this man is a kind person. A person who really *thinks* about what he means."

I still don't understand it. I have no idea why she told me that, because she is a kind person, herself. I can only put it down, nearly three years later, to incredible naiveté on her part. She must have believed—may still believe—that I could merely say the word and change the sexuality of my son, and that I would be well advised to do so. And I cannot think who she could have been referring to. It must have been her father, who is a conservative southern lawyer in Greensboro, North Carolina. And perhaps he is a man of ambiguous sexuality, himself, because otherwise why would it have even crossed his mind as a decision that must be made? But Beth is a sophisticated, worldly woman, and she and her husband count among their closest friends of long standing a number of gay men and lesbians, some of whom are closeted within the community and some of whom are not.

"No, no, Beth. You don't understand. We're really *proud* of Steve for coming out. Steve *wants* a family . . . and he *has* a family. . . ." But my voice rasped over tears, because I hadn't expected to have to explain this to Beth. And that any explanation was necessary to this close friend brought on an overwhelming feeling of hopelessness.

"Oh, Robb! It's so *brave* of you and Charles to handle this so well. It's just amazing to me the things our children put us through. I can't tell you how much I admire you for handling this so well. I hope Stephen appreciates it. I really do. Because I know that in your heart you must really wish that Stephen weren't gay." Her words were slow and melodic with pity and understanding, but her kindly dolefulness on my account—and on Stephen's and Charles's and Jack's—energized me out of my slow slide into melancholy and cast me into full-blown outrage.

"No! For God's sake, Beth! No! I don't wish that even for a minute. I don't wish that even for one single second. I love Stephen! I love Stephen more than you understand. And he *is* gay! It's part of who he is. Why would I want that to change? It would be as absurd as wishing Jack *were* gay." While I was speaking I had leapt up from the chair in surprise at my own self, because I had finally discovered and named exactly what I felt, and I was so relieved to find it out that I could feel myself smiling. I knew I had taken on a childish expression of amazed enlightenment.

"That's very brave—" Beth began, but I interrupted her.

"It's not, Beth. It doesn't have a damned thing to do with bravery."

I didn't say much more to her then, because I didn't have the energy. She has children of her own—wonderful children: two grown daughters and a sixteen-year-old son—and is capable of empathy. Just the other day, when I said to her that I had to be careful not to expect people to understand how passionately I feel about prejudice against gays, she interrupted me. "Perhaps not when you first tell them about your own experience. But you must expect your friends to learn and grow!" And I realized how lucky I have been to have the friends I have.

But when I spoke to her just after my mother-in-law's death I was so unnerved after our conversation that I fled the house and took a long drive up into Vermont, all the way to Manchester. I could drive as fast as I wanted on the short section of interstate that curves through the Green Mountains, which sweep away on either side of the highway. Getting out of the house and away from the phone was consoling.

Manchester has become a mecca for upscale outlet shopping, and I usually avoid the commercial section of town, but I headed straight for it, that afternoon, and parked behind the sleek, many-windowed Ralph Lauren building. I spent several hours browsing through beautiful objects: Coach Leathers, remarkable boots and gadgets at the Orvis Outlet that I presumed was fishing gear, although I don't know anything about fishing. I sorted through antique linens at a shop called Cachet, Icelandic Woolens at Landau, and tried on a coat lined and hooded with Persian lamb at Upland Outfitters. I finally made my way to the Northshire Bookstore, where I only glanced through the huge, sumptuous art books on the front tables by the windows.

It was a soft, sunny day, and I was soothed. I have never enjoyed shopping, particularly, as a pastime, although I don't mind it if I'm headed out with a mission. But I began to understand that afternoon that to wander among so many possible acquisitions is, for a little while, a way to imagine all sorts of other lives you might lead. Listening to two men discuss fly-fishing as they looked over various rods and lures, I pondered for a few minutes the image of myself along the rocky bank of the beautiful Green River, even though I don't know where people go to fly-fish. The remarkable hooded Persian lamb coat made me feel mysterious in a way I know I never have been and never can be. But the heavy slope of the hood against my cheek was seductive. The only purchase I made, though, were two pairs of khakis from J. Crew, for Jack and Stephen, because the slacks had a wonderful slouch to them and a waistband lined with blue-and-white stripes that seemed to me lighthearted.

I drove back slowly, avoiding the interstate and winding along Route 7A. I felt good, and I thought I was calm by the time I got back to Williamstown, making the sharp turn onto Slade Road and driving slowly up the hill. I came to a stop and rolled down my window when I drew abreast of Mary Ann Dupont, who was coming the other way, pushing her little daughter in a stroller. I've always liked Mary Ann, although I don't know her very well.

"How are you?" I said. "I don't think I've seen you all summer. Well, I've seen you from a distance, and Mark stopped by one day to sell me tickets for the school auction. I was amazed at how old he's gotten. It seems such a short time ago that you were pushing him in a stroller. But he said he's almost nine years old."

She smiled at me, and Mary Ann has one of the loveliest smiles of anyone I know, with a dimple appearing just below her cheekbone in a look of softening that is warming to the soul. "He was so excited that you bought five tickets," she said. "He felt responsible when you didn't win anything." She laughed and bent over to check on her daughter and then glanced up at me as she straightened Jessica's sun hat. "But how have you been?"

"Oh, well. Actually it's been sort of a hard week. Charles's mother died. He's down in Georgia right now. But it's been awfully hard on him because some of his relatives are Charismatic Christians. And Charles got into an argument with one of the members of their church about homosexuals. Some woman at my in-laws' house said they are an abomination in the face of God, and, of course, our oldest son—do you remember Stephen? The one with dark hair—came out to us as a gay man a few months ago. So . . . " I shrugged to convey rueful resignation and noticed for the first time that her face had become a perfect blank. She scarcely knows us, and she was probably paralyzed with embarrassment as I babbled on. And I suddenly remembered myself, remembered that I didn't have the right to spread this information, didn't have the right to discuss the intimacies of my husband's family, and certainly shouldn't have peppered this inno-cent bystander with information that I poured out as fast as gunfire.

"Well, I hope everything works out," she said. And I thanked her and drove away, mortified and unable to think of any way to back the car up and explain to her the whole sequence of events that had led me to blurt out the most complex issues of my life to her, when she had probably left her house thinking that it was such a good time to take a nice walk on a summer day.

I went straight into the house and up to the bedroom and picked up the phone once again and telephoned my friends Michael and Louise in New Hampshire. Even while I leafed through my Rolodex to find their number I was thinking about the evening when Michael and Louise and their children met us in Concord, New Hampshire, for a celebratory dinner before Stephen's graduation from St. Paul's School. It had also been a celebration of Louise's birthday. I remembered their young daughters, and how impressed Jack and Stephen had been at what amazingly nice and intelligent and lovely girls the two older children were, and how cute the baby was. When we got back to our motel, Jack had tried to sit as straight as their eldest daughter had sat during the whole of that restaurant meal, but had given up after fifteen minutes.

We had given Louise a collection of small brightly

painted wooden circus animals that could be stacked one on top of another or could stand alone—we had given her a toy, because it was just after the birth of her third child, and we had thought something utterly useless and perfectly whimsical might give her pleasure. And on the occasion of Stephen's graduation, Michael and Louise had taken exactly the opposite tack and given him a sophisticated and quite beautiful atlas of the world, which Charles and I both coveted before Stephen packed it off for his freshman year at Yale.

The restaurant in Concord was ordinary, but the dinner had been delightful because of the company, and just remembering such a pleasurable, comforting event— entirely divorced from the past few weeks when Charles and I had had to accommodate death and the inevitability of unassuagable sorrow—had such an effect on me that I was nearly unable to speak when Michael answered the phone. I hadn't realized how rattled I was.

"Michael, my mother-in-law died," I said.

"Robb?" His voice was fuzzy with static.

"Yes?"

"I'm sorry. I'm outside. I'm on the cordless phone, and . . . wait . . . is that better? Is that clear? What did you say?"

"My mother-in-law died, and Charles is in Atlanta. It's awful for him. He's so sad."

"I'm really sorry, Robb. Could I call him there? Or would that be any help? I'd like to let him know we're thinking about him." The volume of his voice rose and fell through the static.

"Michael, Steve is gay. He came out to us a month

or so ago. And the thing is . . . well, the thing is . . . I don't know what we can do. What Jack will do. He doesn't know yet. I don't know how Steve can be safe. I don't know . . . I'm afraid of the people who will *hate* him now. I don't know how we can protect him. Who we can ever trust again to be our friends. . . . Where we could live—" By then I was speaking over tears.

But Michael was calm and absolutely sincere when he responded. "Robb. Robb," he was polite but insistent at interrupting me. "Don't worry about your friends. You're going to find that some of your friends aren't worth keeping. But don't underestimate Jack. He and Steve are terrific kids. Jack will be fine, and Steve will be fine. You're not going to believe this right now, maybe, but I promise you it's true. Your *own* family is going to be much stronger because of this. You're going to be happy to know Steve better, because Steve is great, and he's going to be just fine."

"But he'll never know . . . he'll never know—" And I don't know what I was planning to say, but Michael interrupted once more.

"And you'll never know what he'll know. And you wouldn't have, no matter what his sexuality was." And I actually laughed, at last, and agreed. And Michael said exactly what I had been hoping all day someone else would know. "Stephen is a wonderful, brilliant, honorable and terrific person. And so is Jack. They are exactly what I hope my own children will grow up to be! Exactly! Steve and Jack and you and Charles are all valuable to each other. You always have been, and this won't change anything. You're all going to be fine. You're all going to be happy again, and this will seem like nothing. I promise you. It's really true. It's really true, Robb."

His voice still wavered in and out of his normal range over the cordless phone, but I could hear him with un-impeachable clarity. And I knew he was right. In fact, as he said it, I knew it's what I had known all along.

Chapter Seven

The
World
of
Outer
Dark

I UNDERSTAND NOW WHAT PEOPLE mean when they talk about a turning point in their lives. It's not as though you were merely walking along straight ahead, thinking you were heading off in the right direction, and then met a barrier and took off briskly the other way. I hadn't known that. Sometimes I think I hadn't known almost anything. The world I had believed I lived in was a more narrowly defined place with

fewer possibilities than the real world actually is. Charles
and I began the long arc of a turn in our lives in which
we began to understand how infinitely complex a thing
it is to be a human being.

Really, the truth of the *complexities* of each human
life was clear as day, once we moved beyond the obstacles
of fear and ignorance that had hindered our vision. We
had lost sight of and forgotten about the fact of each
person's individuality. We had fallen into the habit of
slotting people into neat categories. We had chosen not
to notice that some of them didn't fit, because the act of
categorizing seemed to simplify human negotiations. But
to define humanity so narrowly is to overlook all the
enriching and remarkable complications. Sexuality is only
one facet of personality, and it isn't easily pinned down.
It isn't one thing or another. Sexuality is, in fact, as
intricate, essential, and unique as fingerprints.

And we discovered that there is a quality about grief
that differentiates it from sorrow. Grief is as overwhelming
as joy, and even as you are in its grip you know that
anything so extreme won't last. The moment Stephen had
told us he was gay, both Charles and I had fallen into a
state of grief, but we hadn't acknowledged it. When we
did recognize out loud that we were in a state of *distress,*
we simply put it down to surprise, to worry about
Stephen's well-being, about his future. Both of us instinctively felt that to acknowledge grief would somehow be
a betrayal of Stephen, so we tried to disguise it to ourselves. I know now that we were grieving over the loss
of ourselves as we had assumed we would be immortalized
through the triumphs we had imagined Stephen would

have in his life. We were mourning that repressed but inevitable idea of our own immortality as it was embodied by the idea of Stephen's children and his children's children. And, of course, I know now that Stephen may well have many triumphs, may well have many children, but there is nothing he can do that will grant us immortality.

None of our grief had anything to do with Stephen's sexuality. We had simply been thrown into a state of grief by having to learn in ten minutes what most parents have ten years to absorb—those ten years when their children are between, say, eighteen and twenty-eight. Those ten years when it slowly becomes apparent, in most cases, that their children aren't going to fulfill their parents' every expectation. And I think one of the reasons it is so hard to grasp this elemental fact in one single instant is because well-meaning, enlightened, forward-thinking parents— parents like we thought we were—are really and truly unaware that they are banking on the future they have unconsciously imagined for their children. They are un- willing to believe that they do want more for their chil- dren than their children's happiness. And our expectations were as applicable to the future we imagined for Jack, who is not gay, as that which we had imagined for Stephen.

So Charles and I began the inevitable transition from grief over having our assumptions pulled neatly out from under us to rage at the inequities of society. I thought we had always been enraged at the inequities of society, but until Stephen came out as a gay man, we had never been its victims. Now we understood *exactly* what it felt like to know that you could be denied housing, employment, and equal protection under the law, simply because of who you are. We knew exactly what it felt like to be someone whose very existence makes many people ill at ease at best, and makes others murderously furious at worse. This sudden disempowerment was overwhelming, although only now can I look back and see clearly exactly what was happening to us.

Charles returned from Atlanta as dispirited as I've ever known him to be in his life, and we fell into bad habits brought on by fatigue and unspent, amorphous anger. With Jack and Stephen still in Mexico, the discipline of our summer lives began to unravel, since in academic families it is self-imposed. Neither of us could get any good work done on our writing, and the days were frustrating. We drank too much wine in the evenings; we slept poorly at night; although we depended on each other's company, we were often curt, short-tempered, and unaffectionate toward one another. We had nothing we could do with our rage, and we rarely discussed it because we ended up sleepless and subsumed with generalized fury. It was too heavy a coin to carry with us through all the hours, though, and sometimes we spent small bits of it on each other, but not in its full-blown, thought-out entirety, just little dribs and drabs of petty vexation, irritation, unreasonable crankiness.

My friend Michael sent us the book *Beyond Acceptance: Parents of Lesbians and Gays Talk about Their Experiences*, which I read from cover to cover right away, and which Charles put on his bedside table for a while, because he was still exhausted from what must have seemed to him like the process of becoming orphaned from the family of his childhood.

It's hard for me to believe, now, how astonished I was by *Beyond Acceptance*. And I didn't read it carefully the first time around. It is a collection of interviews of parents of gay men and lesbians, elegantly assembled and with a graceful narration, but I read it greedily and didn't notice with what care it was written, because I was looking for me and Charles and Stephen and Jack. When I browsed through the bibliography I was amazed that so much had been written about having—or being—a gay or lesbian child, and I was simultaneously comforted and chagrined to discover how predictable Charles's and my reaction had been. Also, we had allowed ourselves to slip into a mild state of self-congratulation about what we had assumed up to that point was fairly good behavior on our part. It was hurtful to come face-to-face with the fact that a great many people had behaved far better than we had, and their children quite rightly took it for granted. I suppose I was ignobly disappointed to discover that we were so ordinary, when for years I had considered myself to be especially enlightened and free of prejudice and bigotry. I had thought I was immune to the pitfall of stereotyping, immune to myth and especially to ignorance. The book was humbling.

I found a reference to an organization called P-FLAG—Parents, Families, and Friends of Lesbians and Gays. I worried over the existence of this organization for days before I finally tried to track them down, because I've always been wary of the whole idea of support groups. I didn't want to be someone who needed comfort or solace or support of any kind. But I wasn't any longer in need of comfort, anyway; I wanted information. I still was desperately eager to be able to imagine Stephen's future; I still needed to know if I could ensure his safety. I was terrified of AIDS, and I wanted reassurance, and I was terrified of the casual violence directed at gays, terrified that when men who had been convicted of hate crimes against gays were interviewed in prison, they not only showed no remorse, but thought that, in fact, they were merely carrying out the covert wishes of their communities.

The first person I was in touch with through P-FLAG had had two sons die of AIDS, yet she took my telephone call at work, and she took her lunch break and called me back. She did her best to help me, but I was filled with anguish after she spoke about her sons, who had come out as gay men long before information on the transmission of AIDS had been disseminated. After I hung up I merely sat exactly where I was for over an hour, and I never did mention the call to Charles. I sat there on the side of my bed understanding for the first time that I was not going to get out of my life without experiencing debilitating loss—and not necessarily because of AIDS or because of Stephen. But I had just spoken to a woman who had—in horrifyingly quick succession—lost both her children, yet not only was she back working at a grueling and mind-numbing job, but she had offered to give comfort and information to other people.

I am indebted to her for all sorts of things, but primarily because I think now that my conversation with her helped me—at age forty-four—finish growing up. She directed me to the P-FLAG network that covers the Northeast, and when I contacted them I found much more than comfort, solace, and information; I found a group of people devoted to advocating human and civil rights for their children, siblings, nephews, nieces, grand-children, cousins, parents, or friends. For a while the people in P-FLAG seemed to be the only people among whom Charles and I would ever be completely comfort-able again, because they had gone beyond every possible prejudice. They are people who, late in their lives, dis-covered that they—by virtue of identifying with a person they loved—were part of an unpopular minority or, in a good many cases, *another* unpopular minority.

When I first spoke to Judy, who was the P-FLAG representative nearest me, it was the only time in almost five months that I had spoken to anyone, other than my husband, who understood exactly what I was saying—that I was scared in our society for Stephen, for Jack, for me and Charles, and that a terrible, terrible wrath was over-taking me at the prospect of knowing that we would live out our lives weighed down with the burden of injustice that is visited on gays. I was enraged that we would be subject to the judgment and disapproval of an uninformed society. I was afraid of the scorn and loathing Stephen would be subject to simply because he exists, and I har-bored a nagging fear that somehow Jack and Stephen would lose each other—as if, under any circumstance, I could guarantee the continued affection of siblings.

I was afraid of the sorrow that lay in wait for me and Charles as we grappled with the inexplicable and peculiar loathing of our culture for homosexuals, and—more im-mediate than in our general culture—perhaps we would have to grapple with loathing in our own community. I had not felt such impotent anger or isolation since I was a child with an alcoholic father in an era when alcoholism was considered a character flaw.

Charles and I simply went along day by day. In the evenings we rented mindless teen movies—working our way down from the relatively topflight *Pretty in Pink* and *Adventures in Babysitting,* to *House Party* and *Revenge of the Nerds.* Even so, even choosing such unthreatening videos, we were ambushed by the casual homophobia in nearly every movie we rented, although *Revenge of the Nerds*— not a movie seen by anyone else we know—did seem to us that summer to be a thinly veiled and hopeful allegory about closeted gay life on a mainstream college campus. For all I know, the movie is some sort of underground classic, although probably not, because whatever it's about, it's bad beyond campiness.

That summer when we bought wine in huge jugs and scarcely had a conversation, I think Charles and I both knew that we were in a state of transition. What we knew intellectually—had always known intellectually—had become personal, and so we were in the process of assimilating all this new information viscerally. We were in the process of transforming knowledge into instinct, even though it should have been the other way round. But now I think that much of what we commonly think of as instinct is a combination of knowledge and one's innate sense of justice. And I continue to believe that somewhere at its center the whole of humanity does share a common and innate sense of justice. I hang on to that notion with a kind of religiousness, because otherwise I would be overtaken by despair.

It was a long summer, and we needed to have our children with us again. Charles and I both yearned to have Stephen and Jack back from Mexico and to get on with our family life, however it was going to shape up. When I look back on that stretch of time, it seems to me that we were almost exactly like two of those pins that jugglers use, tossed high up in the air but left suspended. We needed our children back in our lives to ground us.

On the way home from picking up Jack and Stephen at the airport, Stephen was so tired that he dozed off. Jack chatted pleasantly enough, although he, too, was tired, and only later did we get enthusiastic reports of their trip. But at one point Jack said, "Well, all the girls fell in love with Stephen." Charles and I were at such a loss that we didn't respond at all, and I think Stephen must have heard what Jack said, because the next night, fairly late, he leaned into the bedroom where Charles and I were watching a movie about a dog who is lost in the countryside of rural Japan—a Japanese children's movie with English subtitles.

Stephen didn't come all the way into the room, and the expression on his face was neutral. "I wanted to let you know that I just told Jack," he said.

I had wanted him to tell Jack for so long that I was surprised to discover I was filled with apprehension. "Is it okay? Are you both okay?"

"I think it's fine. I think it's going to be okay," Stephen said.

I didn't press him for more information, and I knew enough not to intrude on Jack that evening, since he didn't approach us, but I lay awake all night knowing that if it turned out *not* to be okay, we were facing what to me would be one of the saddest things that could happen in my life: the breaking apart of this remarkable group of people who are my own family.

I got up before dawn because I could hear Jack downstairs in the kitchen. I found him sitting on the counter swinging his long legs so that his heels grazed the cabinets beneath. He looked haggard, and I was afraid of what he might say.

"Jack, are you all right? Is it going to be okay?"

"I'm okay," he said.

"Are you angry at Stephen? Are you upset at him?"

And as he turned to look at me in surprise, his beautiful down-slanted eyes widened just for a moment. "He's my *brother!* I love Steve."

Jack seemed to me to be stunned, and I realized that Stephen had been wiser than I in understanding that he couldn't simply give Jack the information that he was gay and then head off with him for a summer in Mexico. My concern had been that Jack would feel conspired against when he realized that the rest of the family already knew, but Stephen's concern had been that he would lose Jack altogether. Both of us had underestimated Jack, as it turned out, but I think if Stephen had broken the news to Jack at Jack's graduation, it would have skewed their stay at the language institute in Oaxaca. It would have been between them every moment of their trip through-out the rest of the country, distracting them from any other pleasure, even if they didn't speak of it. And in the interim, while the two of them were away, I had done a lot of reading since I discovered there were books on this subject, and I had also done a lot of anticipating.

"Well, does this worry you in any way about your own sexuality?" And Jack just looked at me with a kind of hopelessness at what he must have considered an entirely irrelevant question, although it is often quite relevant, and it is also not uncommon for several siblings in one family to be homosexual. I was determined to take nothing for granted.

"Of course not," he said.

But he was clearly shaken, and what I hadn't taken into account was that in many ways this new information about his older brother was disorienting for Jack in an entirely different way than it had been for me and Charles. I hadn't understood—or I had forgotten—that siblings are absolutely helpless against shaping their lives in some ways around and against the existence of the other.

"No," he said. "I guess it explains a lot of things. Sometimes when I was with Steve and we would see some girl, I would say something to him, and I would just think that I must be so . . . crude. He never said anything. And I just wanted to pick up girls in bars—"

"Oh, Jack! That's a *really* bad idea—" But he shot me a look, and I had the sense to shut up. We didn't say anything for a little while. Jack has a fierce sense of privacy; all his life he has preferred to work his problems out on his own, and I didn't know how to find out if he wanted information or reassurance. But he looked so bleak that I wondered if I should have urged Stephen to tell him at all.

"Would it have been better if Stephen hadn't told you?"

He didn't look at me; he just stared across the kitchen. "That's a really good question," he said, and his voice was soft and uninflected. He wasn't angry, and I couldn't tell if he was sad; I know that he was slightly numb with shock. Everything about his posture was aloof, and it made me feel clumsy and shy of him. I didn't know how to discover how Jack felt; he wanted to mull over the situation on his own. And although I told him to feel free to talk to me or to Charles about anything at all, I knew he wouldn't consult us until he had placed this new development in the context of his own experience.

I went back to bed and lay there remembering vividly the summer when Jack was four years old. I had insisted that Jack and Stephen take a six-week course of beginner swimming lessons, which were held every morning at the YMCA. Jack was particularly recalcitrant, so that every day both of us arrived at the parking lot near tears. I bullied and bribed him into the building, where he sat still as stone at the edge of the pool, his float board strapped around his waist, politely but adamantly refusing to go into the water. By the end of the first week he and I were locked in a battle that I had no chance of winning. In the car after Friday's lesson I broke down in sobs after I buckled the boys into their seats. I sat in the stifling hot car weeping and ranting and banging my fists against the steering wheel for emphasis. Other mothers looked away as they passed by. "Why won't you try it, Jack? Why? Why? Why? Just *try* it! Just try it *one* time!"

In the backseat tears ran down Jack's face, too, but

he answered stoically with no tremor in his voice. "I'm *not* going to take swimming lessons until I *know* how to swim!"

I always have to remember that Jack wants to master his demons, by God, on his own time and by himself. I left him alone and meant not to bring up anything more about Stephen, and Charles did the same. Jack was beginning his first year of college, after all, and he was finally going to be in a co-ed environment. I do remember one bit of advice I gave him before he went off to Wesleyan. "Jack," I said, "you know, if you have any trouble . . . well, I mean, if you're *uncomfortable* or shy about talking to girls, just remember to ask them questions about themselves. Girls are always amazed if boys are interested in their lives. You know, things like where they went to school, what kind of *pets* they have at home, if they have brothers or sisters." Jack was unusually kind and especially tactful for a seventeen-year-old, and he listened politely and smiled. One weekend when he brought home a wonderful girl he had met his first afternoon at registration, she said to me, "That was the *cutest* advice you gave Jack, Mrs. Dew. I told my roommates about it." And she smiled at me fondly.

There wasn't much left of the summer, and it went by in a blur. Our household was peaceful, but I don't remember much else. Or what I do remember are meals shared with unnatural politeness, days spent avoiding debate or discussion, with abundant goodwill on everyone's part toward everyone else, but very little real ease among the four of us. Charles and I remained distant toward our friends—amiable, but aloof.

Stephen was going back early to New Haven to get settled in an off-campus apartment. He was packing the car before I managed to think of a way to ask him a question I needed answered. I approached him as he was sorting through books and papers stored in plastic milk crates. "Listen, Stephen. I don't know what we should do about what we say to people in town."

He was guarded. "I don't see why you have to say anything."

I wanted to be absolutely sure we weren't misunderstanding each other. "Is that what you'd rather we do? I mean, I know it's a small town. . . ."

He stopped sorting through his books and stood up, dusting off his hands on his jeans. "You don't have to feel responsible for me." He spoke calmly, and without irritation. "I don't feel I have to make some sort of statement about being gay."

But *I* became irritated, because we were talking around each other. "No, Steve. That's not what I mean. I mean this in just a practical way. Your father and I are fine. We don't feel a bit . . . *sorry* you're gay! We don't regret anything about you—"

"Oh, come on!" Finally he was angry, but when he challenged me I was pleased to realize that I was telling the truth.

"God dammit, Stephen! Give us a little credit! But I don't want to make *your* life difficult. I don't want to reveal anything about you that you would rather keep private. I mean, when someone asks me if you're still going out with Chloe, or if you have a new girlfriend—"

"You want to know if I want to stay in the closet in

Williamstown?" He sounded simultaneously resigned and disheartened.

Stephen and I regarded each other for a moment— not angrily, because by then I was at a loss to explain what I was getting at.

"No," I said. "Or maybe that *is* what I mean. But not for *us*. I don't know what you want." Even as I spoke I realized that I was not being completely frank. I hadn't hit upon any comfortable way to break the news to my friends or acquaintances; I hadn't figured out any easy way to challenge their assumptions.

"But this is just what I've spent most of my life trying to keep you and Dad from having to face!" I have rarely seen Stephen look as stricken as he did when he suddenly blurted that out, his voice becoming large and hollow, his brows drawn down and his mouth rigid with strain. "It would be easier for me if you *did* tell people," he said. He turned away, gazing at the street, and I didn't speak for a moment, because he seemed to be considering what else he wanted to say. But I saw his shoulders relax, and I was surprised to realize that something had amused him. All at once he was no longer anguished, but amused and wry. "I mean, I've never figured out the etiquette for this."

And he fell into a pantomime of the unaggressive posture of amiability that most people adopt when they first meet someone. "Hi! Stephen Dew," he said, with an upward inflection on "Dew," and smiled beamingly at the air in front of him, extending his hand in greeting to an imagined new acquaintance, replete with a quick downward nod of the head as he reached out—an attitude of succinctly making oneself known as unthreatening while simultaneously staking a claim to one's own existence. "Good to meet you." He was shaking hands with the nonexistent stranger, and I found myself grinning, because Stephen's a good mimic. He has a knack for catching telling gestures.

"Yeah," he said, mocking the typical give-and-take of first meeting someone and exchanging pleasantries and necessary information. "I'll be in my junior year. No, Yale. Right. Thank you. It *is* a great school, I think. Um huh. That's true. New Haven *is* dangerous. No, I'm in Calhoun College, but I have some friends in Jonathan Edwards."

I relaxed too, and laughed. Stephen and Jack will both sometimes go into a sketch of some little bit of trivia from their lives that explains more to me about what they are like than any amount of discussion between us. I love these little synopses of contemporary life, and I watched as Stephen remained attentive to the hail-fellow-well-met he had conjured up out of thin air.

"An English major," he said earnestly. "Right! I'm definitely planning on a life of poverty," he said, with another quick nod of his head, and I laughed. Invariably, whenever my sons reveal to someone that they're English majors, the same hearty witticisms are hauled out—something along the lines of "Nothing like a good Ivy League education to get you ready for the real world! You're planning to starve in a garret, I guess. Sit in coffee shops and make tomato soup out of hot water and ketchup?" And Stephen and Jack laugh politely to preserve the other person's dignity.

Stephen withdrew his hand and stood smiling and

nodding at his foolish but well-meaning imaginary new acquaintance. "Nope, no one I'm really serious about. No, no. No girlfriend. Well, in my case, no *boy*friend, actually. That's right. Yes, gay. And you?"

We both laughed, and Stephen shrugged as if to say, "You see."

"Are you sure though, Steve? It feels like invading your privacy."

"But you don't get to have any privacy if you're gay and come out. Your life is immediately everybody's property. Everybody likes gossip. But people are more comfortable if you stay in the closet. Most gays at Yale *do* stay in the closet." He had grown serious. "But you and Dad don't have to feel responsible for any of this. You shouldn't do anything that makes you feel uncomfortable."

I have spent too much of the energy of my life accommodating other people. Not in large ways, and not the people I love deeply. But a million times, perhaps, I have deferred outwardly while privately disagreeing. I thought I was acting out of a heightened sense of delicacy, but those people with whom I refused to disagree I merely wrote off, didn't see again, avoided at parties, until there were so many people I had acceded to that I simply avoided parties.

Earlier that week Stephen happened to be in the room when I was placing a catalogue order over the phone, although I wasn't paying attention to him.

"No, two 'B's," I said. "R–O–B–B. Oh, don't worry, it's not your fault. You can blame my parents. A family name. Right! Great! Okay. The middle name is Forman with no 'E.' No, in the middle. F-O-R-M-A-N. Right. And the last name is Dew. D-E-W. No, not 'Drew.' Dew. Like the morning dew. Oh, no! Don't worry about it. *Everyone* finds it confusing! The first item number I want to order is—What? No, Robb Forman Dew is *my* name. My husband is *Charles* Dew. Oh, I know it's pretty strange. Yes, people get it mixed up all the time. Okay. The address is 424 *Slade* Road, with a "D," Williamstown—which is one word spelled exactly like it sounds— Massachusetts. No, that's 'M.A.' Right, right. Well . . . yes, Slate Road. S-L-A-T-E." I pushed on, giving my credit card number, ordering several items, and wishing the operator well before I got off the phone. But when I hung up I noticed Stephen's face was fixed in an expression of disapproval.

"What's the matter? Were you waiting to ask me something? I was busy. What do you need?"

"No, I don't need anything. But why do you do that? It's not your job to make the operator's life easy. You could expect her to pay attention."

"Well, good lord, Stephen. That's hardly any of your business. Why do you care?"

"I don't care about that. But you even let them spell the name of the street wrong—"

"Don't worry about it. They always get almost every part of our name and address wrong, and especially our zip code. But eventually it arrives." I wasn't paying much attention, and I was amiably reassuring Stephen, so I was surprised when it was clear he was still irritated.

"Why do you let them get away with that?"

I was suddenly irritated myself, and defensive. "Why

in the world do you care? It's just an order for a shower
curtain from The Vermont Country Store. It's not for
you, anyway! It'll get here just fine."

"I don't care about that. I mean, that's not what . . .
that's not the point. You're always afraid you're going to
hurt someone's feelings, and so you never . . . *insist* that
they just get it right. You never stick up for yourself."

I was astonished. "What? How can you say that? Of
course I stick up for myself!"

"You don't. And then the people who don't understand what you're doing . . . You end up hating the
people who don't realize you've let them say something
you think is really stupid."

"Stephen! Give me a break! That was a telephone
operator who probably takes hundreds of orders a day. I
don't think she's stupid. I don't care about her one way
or another. I certainly don't *hate her*—"

"Not her. She's just . . . It's not important. It's nothing." And he let it drop, but I was left perplexed and
surprised. All of a sudden, though, I understood his ob-
jection, and I understood that he wasn't really lecturing
me; he was trying to figure out what conduct would be
best for himself. It is possible that he was just in a bad
mood and that the unctuous manner I *do* fall into in the
face of officiousness annoyed him just as it annoys Charles
and Jack. But whatever prompted his remark, it crossed
my mind that Stephen would enjoy a non-adversarial
relationship with the world as much as anyone, but to
some degree he had forfeited his chance for that just by
the act of coming out. An entirely easy relationship with
the world was too high a price to pay if it meant he had

to sacrifice his own identity. And I'm lifting a page from his book; I've gotten fed up, too, with comporting myself to ensure other people's comfort. I'm sick to death of being "sweet."

There are any number of closeted gays and lesbians in Williamstown, but many of them are only in what my friend Jay Lager once described as a "glass closet." Ever since I heard that phrase I've had a mental picture—a snapshot idea—of a closet constructed of one-way mirrors, with the occupant only able to see himself. He can never know when someone else is peering in, so that every moment of his life must be self-conscious and considered. For too long, society has demanded this pretense from gays because it is comfortable for the majority, but it must be excruciating—and is sometimes deadly—to anyone trapped inside. The idea of our own family being confined in such a space was appalling. So when I was asking Stephen how he wanted us to handle the fact that he had come out as a gay man, and he assured me that he didn't want Charles or Jack or me to feel we had to do anything at all, that we shouldn't feel we had to do anything that would make us uncomfortable, I discovered I was indignant.

"You don't understand, Stephen," I said, when I realized that he was worrying about our peace of mind. "We're really mad. We're *really* mad!" And I was surprised that my voice became loud and declaratory. "We're just furious that you *ever* had to be in the closet! We're *furious* that we didn't have more sense! That we must have caused you so much pain. That we're *surrounded* by ignorance! It's really just time that everyone . . . grows *up* for God's sake! It's like our whole society is caught up in some awful state of junior high school obsession. . . . Stupid, prurient, smarmy sort of whispering. . . . I'm sick of it! I'm just sick to death of it! My God! We're only talking about sex and love!"

Stephen seemed startled, and I was surprised myself at my own vehemence. Charles and I are generally reflective, but during this period of our lives we sometimes found ourselves spontaneously articulating beliefs at the moment of encompassing them, and now and then we astonished ourselves. I calmed myself and spoke less urgently. "If you're absolutely sure it's okay with you, then we want to be out of the closet, too. And I know Jack. . . . Jack would refuse absolutely. . . . He wouldn't *ever* prefer to pretend. . . . Well, maybe if you asked him, but it would infuriate him to feel he had to hide anything about you."

CHARLES AND I WERE THROUGH WITH SORROW. We became official P-FLAG representatives, which only meant that we were listed as a phone contact in our area for anyone who got in touch with the national office looking for help or information. We also began sending information to local doctors, schools, and churches. When asked, Charles gave an interview to our local paper, and we alerted the Bisexual, Gay, and Lesbian Union at Williams College to the fact that P-FLAG existed. We did our best to help those who called, or at least to put them in touch with someone else who could help them.

Williams College, in an attempt to strengthen ties between the community and the institution, has a unique

policy of matching funds—at a one- to four-dollar ratio—
that any of its employees donate to designated charities in
the three small towns where most of their employees live.
In Williamstown, the college will match funds to the
Community Chest, which sponsors any number of desperately needed agencies, such as the Village Ambulance
Service, Community Day Care, and various other carefully chosen organizations, including, unfortunately, The
Boy Scouts of America. In 1991 the BSA had issued a
nasty reaffirmation of their policy to discriminate against
openly gay boys or men in every aspect of scouting, and
Charles and I were angry that Williams College was helping to support them, but we assumed it was inadvertent.

I have learned by now that you must always start at
the top, but I was naive then, assuming that educated
people are also tolerant and enlightened. After being
fobbed off from one office to another, I finally reached an
administrator at Williams who thought he could help me,
but by that time I was exasperated though still cordial.

"I am calling to find out," I said, pleasantly, "if
Williams College intends to donate funds on a matching
basis through the Community Chest to the Boy Scouts?"

"Yes," he said. "We're very pleased we finally got
the matching funds program in place. We're quite proud
of it. It's a way to maintain a healthy tie between the
college and the town."

I was nonplussed. I realized that he thought I was
eager to increase my donation to the Boy Scouts. "But
the Boy Scouts refuses to allow gay men or boys to
participate in scouting," I said, but I know my voice

wasn't assertive, because I was unnerved by his satisfaction with the whole idea.

"Well . . . ," and he paused for just a moment, "I'm sure you've heard about incidents of Scoutmasters molesting young boys—"

"No, no. You're missing my point, I'm afraid. You're talking about pedophilia. Ninety-five percent of pedophiles are grown men who molest young girls. I'm talking about *gay* adolescents and openly gay men who want to work with the Scouts because they care deeply about scouting. Because it's meant a lot to them in their lives," I said, but still with a note of surprise and probably even slight supplication in my voice. "You see, this concerns me very much, because our son came out as a gay man, and, naturally, we oppose Williams' policy of contributing matching funds to any organization that discriminates against *anyone*."

He backpedaled as fast as he could, assuring me that he would look into it right away and would be in touch with the Community Chest. Not until the following year, when we challenged the Community Chest for continuing to support an organization that discriminates against homosexuals, did we discover that the Williams College administrator I had spoken with had never brought it to their attention. He had never mentioned our complaint to anyone as far as we know, and yet Williams College already had in place a policy of nondiscrimination on the grounds of sex, sexual orientation, race, national or ethnic origin, color, religion or creed, age, disability, or status as a disabled or Vietnam-era veteran.

The second time around, Charles went straight to Frank Oakley, who was then the president of the college, and who was responsible for adding the policy of nondiscrimination on the grounds of sexual orientation in the first place. And when Charles and I finally met with the board of the Community Chest, they seemed genuinely taken aback at the harshly worded policy of The Boy Scouts of America. The college administrator with whom I had spoken early on had never informed them of our complaint, and I am still astonished at the sheer political stupidity of his actions. I suspect that had it been Charles who initially contacted him he would have behaved quite differently, but I can't ever know that for sure. I think he is a decent man; he's been in touch with me recently and has become better educated on the whole issue of gay rights.

After a failed attempt to get the local Great Trails Council to renounce the policy, the Community Chest withdrew funding of the BSA with a unanimous vote. But so much ill will was stirred up over the matter that we got nasty phone calls in the middle of the night, angry letters appeared in the paper, and we found it worthwhile to pay a tidy sum to get unlisted phone numbers.

It was an unsettling time, although it was good training in learning what to expect. There is a professor at the college whose children grew up with mine who—because of our role in the Boy Scout issue—not only doesn't acknowledge me and Charles when we pass on the street, but, unforgivably, refuses to acknowledge Stephen, who was never a Scout, who had nothing to do with our taking on the issue, save being gay and eventually coming out, and who has been a loyal friend to that professor's child. Charles is a good-natured man, but when he first saw this professor purposely ignore Stephen, he came home in such a murderous mood that I was afraid he would challenge the man when he saw him next, and that wouldn't have served any purpose at all.

We lost respect for some people we had considered good friends and gained friends where we assumed we would meet resistance. As a result of all the publicity, we were invited to speak at local churches and schools and to the Athletic Department at Williams College, because they were concerned about charges of insensitivity toward gay athletes. Charles did most of the public speaking, because I've always found it excruciating and am not very good at it, but every time we did address a public forum we felt better. It seemed to us that we were doing the best we could, that we were helping a little bit, and finally we were able to get back to our own work with revived concentration.

We also informed the rest of our far-flung family. And every time I broke the news to someone else I was reminded of the little tableau of the failure of etiquette Stephen had enacted. We didn't insist on talking about Stephen's sexuality, but it usually came up as a response to someone else's assumption that he was heterosexual, or was the answer to the question of why we were involved with P-FLAG, and, more often than I would like, it was the response to a casually smug homophobic joke or remark.

My mother and sister were wonderful, because it really didn't matter at all to them, and that's rare, although many people had the grace to pretend that it didn't catch them off guard. I had to remind myself constantly that my friends and acquaintances were unlikely to be at the same stage I was, although amazingly often people would say to me that their brother, or son, or sister, or father, or mother was gay or lesbian.

I am still angry and amazed that when I merely gave some people the information that my son is gay, they were under the impression that they had the right to an opinion about it. On a profound level, *anyone's* opinion of homosexuality is beside the point. His or her opinion of the fact of homosexuality is as relevant as my opinion of the sun or the moon. And it still dumbfounds me when those people I assumed understood this without question betray their ignorance.

Not long ago, on a rainy December afternoon in 1993, one of Charles's colleagues—a member of the Williams College faculty—said to me that one of her students had gone to New York and become gay because it was the politically correct thing to do. And that day, for the first time in my life, I really understood the inherent exhaustion and resigned despair of any member of a minority group who insists on being accorded dignity.

I despaired of that woman as soon as those words came out of her mouth. If she could believe something as foolish as that, given her education and the information to which she has access, she may lack the ability to empathize. On the other hand, the couple who come in two hours a week to help us clean—when they asked what I was writing—congratulated our whole family. "You've got really great kids," Julie said. "They're two of the nicest guys I know! Isn't it awful that so many people are so hateful? Who are *they* to judge anybody else!"

One day not so long ago, when I was talking with the black writer Gloria Naylor and telling her about this book, she made a low sound of inclusion, of acknowledgment. "Ummm. So, really, Robb, you know what it's like to be a minority, now." And I agreed.

I also understood what another black writer, a woman who lives nearby, meant when she said to me, "Well, I'll march with you. I mean it. I'll march with you anytime. I used to always be caught in traffic by the Gay Pride march with my sister-in-law when we were going back to New York, and we would sit and watch, and we would say to each other, 'There we'll be. That's where we'll be. Marching with our signs with the other parents.' That's what we'd say. Now, though, I have these children. Mixed race and Jewish! I have these three children living here in the middle of nowhere, and I don't know what they might be suffering. But sometimes I think maybe now . . . I mean, not just anyone can have a black child, but anyone can have a gay child."

I am so grateful to both those women who didn't condemn me for something they had always understood about me and of which I hadn't been conscious—my ease in our particular society because I was born white in a Protestant family. But I've thought about what they said, and it's not quite applicable—the comfort of shared experience they offered me. Because a child who is black or Latino or Asian presumably lives in a family made up of the same ethnic group, or at least lives in a family all too aware of the difficulties involved in being a part of that minority group. But gay children grow up alone. They aren't part of any group, least of all do they feel they are like the others in their own family.

And so I was relieved when Charles's brother said to me that, when Charles told him about Stephen, he felt reassured that the family could still work—could hold together as a family—even without my mother-in-law at the helm.

I wrote a long letter, and sent booklets and pamphlets from P-FLAG, to St. Paul's School, asking them to get involved on some level and address the issue of sexual orientation and isolation and discrimination, and Charles wrote a similar letter to the new headmaster at Woodberry Forest School, and he also wrote a private, personal letter to Daniel Elgin, who had been Jack's advisor and had worked closely with Charles when Charles was on the board. We worried and debated and anguished over the wording and message of those letters, and we mailed them off with cautious hopefulness.

But whatever societal tension we were dealing with, the mood among the four of us was pretty cheerful, because both boys phoned us fairly often with news of how their lives were going, and they stayed in touch with each other. Jack and Stephen were each involved in their first long-term relationships. Stephen was still seeing the Yale student he had referred to when we were having breakfast together in Virginia during the week of Jack's graduation. A young man named David whom I had hoped was from a good family. Jack had become pretty deeply involved with Laura, the Wesleyan student he had brought home in the early fall.

Charles and I went down to visit both boys at once on a fall day that *wasn't* parents' weekend, so we would have more time with them than if we had to keep up with a hectic schedule of school-planned activities. I had left a message on Jack's phone machine that we would pick him and Laura up at Wesleyan and drive on to New Haven to meet Stephen for lunch, and I came home to find a message on my machine from Jack in return. He sounded exasperated. "I hope you remembered to tell Stephen to invite David to come with us," he said. I had, indeed, but as soon as I heard that message, I knew that the four of us would be all right.

During lunch at a pleasant restaurant in New Haven, I was enormously cheered by how much I liked the people my children had chosen to be involved with. I understand in retrospect that my liking them was just very good luck. Parents don't get to choose who their children love, and Laura and David are no longer involved with Jack and Stephen, although I think they're all still friends. But I know it might have set us back a good deal, at this fledgling stage of getting to know our grown children, had Laura or David—especially David—been determined to challenge our early and fragile idea of ourselves as open-minded, enlightened parents. Laura and David were attractive people in every way in which that can be understood. Everyone seemed to be comfortable. Stephen and Jack began to teasingly recount the peanut butter sandwich story, and David leapt to my defense.

"At least your mother made your sandwiches *for* you. I had to make my own."

"You're a man after my own heart, David," I said.

And he was. I was immediately fond of the two strangers at our table. It seemed exactly right to me that my children would be involved with them. Only briefly was I sad when I understood that David and Stephen didn't take for themselves the affectionate intimacy—a touch on the shoulder, a tendency to lean toward the other one in an obvious inclusion that embodied a quality of tenderness—that Jack and Laura fell into unthinkingly. On the other hand, I realized that if Stephen and David exhibited any signs of affection toward each other, they might actually endanger themselves, and that was a thought I conveniently held apart from the moment of being together with all those people I liked so much.

That afternoon I chose not to think about a second conversation I had had months earlier with Stephen when I pressed him once again about Charles and my revealing to our friends in town, to our relatives all over the country, the fact that he was a gay man. We had been sitting at the kitchen table at breakfast, just the two of us, and Stephen was reading the paper.

"Are you absolutely sure that *our* coming out won't infringe on your privacy?" I asked. "Won't make you uncomfortable when you're here in Williamstown?"

He put the paper down and glanced at me with an expression that didn't succeed in disguising his irritation. "Mom. We've talked about this. But you really don't understand. I mean, you don't understand that when you make the decision to come out, to stop pretending and keeping tabs on everything you've said . . . , well, you're also making the decision to live the rest of your life as a

. . . as if you're at *war*. I don't mean in any political way
or melodramatic way. What I mean is that you always
have to know that the next person who knows you're gay
may want to kill you."

"Stephen!"

He frowned in frustration. "No, I don't mean they'll
try to kill you. But they might really wish you didn't exist.
So just the decision not to pretend to be someone I'm not
was also a decision to be . . . on guard the rest of my life."
And then he suddenly became angry, his hands tightening
into fists as they rested on the discarded newspaper and
his voice becoming fuller. "Because I refuse to be ghet-
toized. I don't want to be pushed to the literal edges of
the earth. Provincetown. The Keys. San Francisco. Nothing seems more depressing to me than giving up the life
I want because of fear. I have a *right* to live my life in the
world!" His face relaxed then into a quizzical expression;
his voice softened. "And I don't see why anyone cares. It
seems so strange to me that people would just hate me in
the abstract."

And I didn't ask him anything, because I couldn't
bear to know more than that just then. And I won't ever
know more from Stephen. Whatever has happened to
him, or if he has suffered harassment, is a matter he will
keep to himself. I don't know all that Stephen wants from
his life, but I know he doesn't want to be remarkable or
endangered because of whom he might love. Who among
us does? But at that lovely lunch in New Haven, where
Charles and I were so happy for our children, I pushed
everything threatening out of my head.

The six of us were crowded at a round table probably meant for four, and toward the end of the meal we were joined by several other friends of Stephen's at Yale, and we made room and offered dessert. The conversation grew loud and lively and turned to movies—well, not movies, but *films*—although Charles and I found ourselves in a debate with each other over the merits of *House Party* versus *House Party II*. All at once we realized that silence had fallen around the table, and we looked up to discover the whole group of our children and our children's friends looking at us in embarrassed disbelief, and then they laughed good-naturedly, because they thought we were kidding, and we weren't fools enough to tell them otherwise. Charles and I came home feeling that if we had met the two people with whom our children would spend the rest of their lives, then we could count ourselves lucky, although our sons were pretty young for that to be likely.

We were feeling hopeful all around, really. So many people in Williamstown reassured us. One afternoon when I went into Jane's Berkshire Greenhouse to buy flowers for a dinner party, the woman who owns the shop came up and gave me a hug. "I think it's great that you're doing what you're doing," she said. "Tommy and I grew up being activists, but even our kids think you're doing a good thing to speak out." It was nice to hear, not because we wanted credit for anything we were doing, but because it was always a relief to know we weren't being disapproved of behind our backs. But I'm sure there were and are any number of people who disapprove of our taking on this issue. One friend asked me why it was necessary to bring up Stephen's sexuality at all. "After all, Robb," she said, "*straight* people aren't always throwing information about their sex lives in your face. I just think that this whole idea of *celebrating* one's sexuality is a bit much."

As it happens, I find this particular remark unusually offensive, condescending, and smug. "But, Denise! I saw you put your hand on Stuart's arm at the reception at Mount Hope Farm! You leaned over and whispered something to him. It was *very* suggestive. I would have to say it seemed to me that you were absolutely *flaunting* your heterosexuality!" I was surprised at myself, because my voice deliberately mimicked incredulity. I was making it obvious that I was being disingenuous. I felt my face flush, but I was angry beyond backing away from this confrontation, and I had learned by then that if I let a remark like Denise's go by, then I would feel terrible for days, sick with anger and shame. "And you're over fifty years old, aren't you? So it's not about *procreation!*"

She and I stepped away from each other, each of us aghast—I because I am horrified by awkwardness, embarrassment, or any public disagreement; and she because she really had no idea how deeply she had offended me, and also because in my previous life people assumed—rightly—that I would cover for them if they insulted me. I had been someone who would do almost anything to avoid unpleasantness. She was angry that I had fallen out of character.

"Well, but that's all *natural.* You're being absurd, Robb. You can't expect to change society."

"Well, for God's sake, Denise. Of *course* you can. If

it weren't possible to change society, *you* wouldn't have the right to vote!"

Gloria Naylor and my writer friend who lives nearby, and various other friends and colleagues who don't live in Williamstown are important allies, but Charles and I are communal creatures and require more than the support of the far-flung assortment of people we admire but who, for the most part, don't know Stephen. If we were going to be required to maintain an elaborate pretense in order to be comfortable within our community of neighbors— the people who run the market, my friend who is also the woman who cuts my hair, the owners of the greenhouse, the contractor who is renovating our garage—then we would have to leave.

Charles and I had had long and serious conversations about relocating to various places where we would be anonymous. He had just finished the first draft of a book that was the culmination of twenty years of painstaking research, and I could write wherever I lived. We had decided that in a few years he could take early retirement, and we could move if need be. We were going to do our best to remain in the community we loved, in the house we had spent such ardent energy restoring, among friends we had cherished. But if those friends refused to be real allies of our redefined family, then we would pick up and go. If we could not unselfconsciously express our pleasure in being the parents of our own children among all these people in Williamstown who are far more than acquaintances, then we would move away. Of course we would regret any relocation; it would disturb us deeply, but it was the obvious and easiest alternative to staying on if we were disapproved of. We weren't as valiant or as young as Stephen. We thought we were too old to begin to live our lives as if we were at war.

That was during the winter of 1992, when I had realized just in that conversation with Denise that I did indeed intend to challenge society in the matter of its acceptance of gays, although I intended to do what I could at a local level, and within a limited forum. Charles and I were both busy writing, and with Stephen and Jack happy in their lives and settled at school, we were comfortable with, and even a little proud of, our ongoing personal and local crusade for human and civil rights for gays and lesbians. We were happy to be involved with P-FLAG, and it didn't occur to us for quite a while that we weren't really doing very much at all except the simple, decent, responsible job of advocating for and supporting our own son.

Chapter Eight

Family
Values—
Valuable
Families

A S IT HAPPENED, coming out of our own closet was an enormous relief. Whenever it's necessary to engage in deception in order to keep a secret, it's a good bet that you are indulging in a bit of concealment that is damaging to the soul—the idea of keeping silent is inevitably transmogrified to an emotion akin to shame.

Probably we are the subject of some controversy in town, but for the most part I don't think anyone is very interested in our lives one way or another. Our society *is* growing up, becoming more sophisticated, more at ease with diversity even while it wrestles with the backlash to the acknowledgment of that diversity.

When I was growing up in the South, so much was considered inappropriate for discussion that I didn't even know, until I was twenty years old, that the Holocaust had taken place. Certainly no one ever mentioned homosexuality, although I realize, thinking back on it, that several of my parents' friends were gay, lesbian, or bisexual. I have no idea if anyone ever said so, but my guess is that it was general knowledge that remained unmentioned. But that intention of tactful silence does terrible damage to the person on whose behalf it's being exercised.

And the damage of secretiveness radiates outward, in an attempt to preserve the pretense of heterosexuality. In a marriage, for instance, in which one partner is a closeted gay or lesbian, there is often great distress caused to the other spouse and any of the couple's children, who intuitively know that something's amiss and conspire instinctively to keep up appearances. Although baffled and uninformed, they act to bolster the relationship at great cost to the family's mental health.

Charles and I have made a remarkable number of new friends in Williamstown since we came out of the closet. We've reinforced and strengthened former friendships and find that we are delighted to be able to live in a place where we have no need to keep secrets. We also have let some strained friendships fall by the wayside, but I think those were friendships that wouldn't have held up over the long haul in any case. Little by little we inched forward through the year, past Christmas and into 1992, thinking less and less about relocation, not feeling the need to retreat into anonymity, thinking of ourselves as being at home.

I irritate my New England friends by my fervent embrace of January and February—they dread those two months, and I long for them all through the year because I know they are the time of my most productive activity. In November and December, during the frenzy of the holidays, which I revel in and need, I also am reassured as the daylight fades so early, often before I return home from afternoon errands. I'm never bothered by the short-ened days, because in the early dark will come first the celebration of the holidays and then the slide into the brief, spare, stern days of winter. The slatelike days of January and February fall one upon another with a kind of severity that offers no distraction of any kind. Winter in New England is an earnest season, and it instills in me a puritanical discipline that I am hard pressed to measure up to in more temperate months.

I began work on a new novel, and both Charles and I continued reading and talking and educating ourselves about the real nature and range of human sexuality. Charles and I answered P-FLAG calls and handled them with as much skill as we could. We did suffer setbacks now and then to our fairly fragile peace of mind. We were temporarily devastated when we received a letter from John Grinalds, the headmaster of Woodberry Forest School, briefly thanking us for our letter to him, but telling us that he wouldn't consider any sort of educational program about homosexuality at Woodberry Forest. He wrote us that there had never been an incident of homo-sexuality at Woodberry Forest School.

And we only recently had a reply to our letter to Daniel Elgin, Jack's former advisor. It was a sad letter and a careful letter. He said he hadn't written because he hadn't understood that a response was expected until he had heard from me a second time, and he also said that he would not lie to his friends, and that he had nothing hopeful to report. He sees no prospect of John Grinalds's rethinking the issue of homosexuality, which Mr. Grinalds, as a born-again Christian, considers a sin.

Just this past week I took another look at the school's catalogue. It says in part: "Established on Christian principles, Woodberry Forest School maintains no formal church ties, yet the school believes that all facets of personal development must be based on spiritual and ethical awareness." What could be less ethical than insisting that a young person lead his whole life as a lie, turning all his energy toward maintaining the appearance of heterosexuality? I am continually baffled by the reluctance of people of the most honorable intentions to fail to point out that anyone's opinion of homesexuality is utterly beside the point. But Daniel also wrote that his position at the school prohibits him from speaking out, and that the necessity of remaining silent causes him pain.

Daniel Elgin is a wonderful man, but his silence on this issue disappoints me, because he doesn't understand, or won't act upon, the fact that he can, in fact, speak out. Breaking silence is always an option, even though it's true that it's an option that may have unpleasant consequences. We are still worried about the fate of any young man at Woodberry Forest School who might be wrestling with his sexuality. A good friend of Jack's, who was in the class ahead of his, came out just this past year. John Grinalds may not believe there have been any *incidents* of homosexuality, but whether he chooses to acknowledge it or not, there certainly are young men at the school who are gay but have no one to talk to, no apparent role model, and perhaps no idea that their situation is not unique. Charles and I are deeply worried about the welfare of these boys. The statistics of suicide for gay teens is terrifying, and it's dangerously irresponsible for enlightened school administrators, counselors, and teachers to remain silent.

The reaction from St. Paul's School was equally disappointing, and our family has been contacted by many of their gay and lesbian alumni who feel they are being ignored by their alma mater, and who are disheartened about their own school, because the headmaster, David Hicks, is a man of strongly held, ultraconservative beliefs. In the two conversations I have had with him, he struck me as hysterically homophobic and backward thinking on almost every social issue. Many St. Paul's alumni—both straight and gay—who have been in touch with me are directing their funds to public and private schools that have adopted sound, progressive policies and programs to promote understanding and lessen harassment and hatred of gays and lesbians.

But, also, the very idea of "family" in modern society is a complicated thing, often comprising much more than actual blood relations. If you entrust a child to the care and guidance of a school when that child is only fourteen

years old, then the institution itself becomes literally familiar. When the headmasters of Woodberry Forest and
St. Paul's School turned a cold shoulder on us, we could
only feel it as a rebuff of us by the entire community they
represent, even though we know that both our sons are
remembered with great fondness by many faculty members at their respective schools, and we know that there
are faculty members of both schools who are hoping for
and working toward policy changes within their institu-
tions.

But Charles and his older brother both went to
Woodberry Forest School; they both excelled there, and
they both hold it in great affection, as does Jack. In fact,
Charles has a rare, valuable, and probably unequaled library of southern history, which he had wanted to see
housed at the school. Now, of course, he would never
entrust the school with such a gift. So there is real sorrow
in this stalemate for the two of us. It has been, in its own
way, one more loss of family.

Our own emergence from the closet was a peculiar
time; sometimes it seemed to us that we were divorcing
our own past. But the real tragedy is the fact that those
two headmasters, who are supposedly devoted to the
highest ideals of education, have adamantly refused to be
further educated themselves, and therefore have put the
welfare of many of their students at risk.

AS THE FACT OF STEPHEN'S SEXUALITY became less
and less remarkable to us, we found that we were taking
giant steps in our progress toward our own future, and

while we occasionally hit a brick wall, we also had moments of grace and real joy. One day Sally Henderson phoned me and seemed to be having difficulty articulating her reason for calling. I was caught off guard and initially filled with misgivings. I had always liked the Hendersons, although I only knew them casually, through my children. Their oldest son, Alex, was at Yale with Stephen, although not in the same year, but the two of them were in the same residential college and had become friends.

When Alex and Stephen had brought a huge coed group of their friends to Williamstown for two nights during winter break, they had split up between our two houses, and Sally and I had enjoyed comparing notes afterwards. Sally's husband, Jim, was one of the pediatricians who took care of my children when they were small, and I had always liked him. The more Charles and I had seen of the Hendersons, while Alex and Stephen were at Yale, the more we enjoyed getting to know them, and we began to think of them as real friends. We knew they were aware that Stephen had come out as a gay man—Stephen's friend, David, had, in fact, been their son Alex's roommate—but we had never really discussed it.

Sally seemed so awkward and flustered for the first few minutes on the phone that I immediately assumed she wanted to talk about something she thought I wouldn't want to hear.

"I don't quite know how to ask you this, Robb. I don't want to seem to be presuming . . . this might be something that you should check with Steve. I feel uncomfortable letting Timothy . . . well, I told him I thought I ought to check with you."

Timothy is the Henderson's youngest son, and I couldn't imagine what was troubling Sally that could have to do with Stephen. I didn't say anything, and after a moment she continued.

"Timothy has been working on his essay for his prep school applications, and he's finished it. I wasn't going to read it, because it ought to be his work. But I just couldn't stand it, and I decided I should at least look it over in case he had taken the whole thing too casually, or something. But after I read it I thought that I really should check with you before he sent it."

"You did? Why?"

"Well, you know, Timothy has always liked Steve so much. . . ." I didn't know what she was getting at, and when she came to another pause I just waited. "Well, you know, we didn't think there was any reason not to tell Timothy when Steve came out to Alex. And Timothy was surprised. Well, what he's written his essay about is that he hadn't understood, really, what homophobia was . . . and how cruel and wrong homophobia is, until one of his favorite of his brother's friends came out as a gay man."

I hadn't realized until I was standing there in the kitchen holding the phone to my ear that, even though we had gotten much encouragement from local people, I had been harboring a vague, defensive grudge against the whole of Williamstown. I had been expecting disapproval, expecting narrow-minded unkindness. We had developed the hypersensitivity to insult common to almost every embattled minority, and it is essential for members of those minorities to keep their antennae up, their radar highly tuned; it is a survival technique, but it takes an emotional toll.

We were easily offended by the unthinking homophobia that is sadly pervasive in the transactions of everyday life. But we tried to take into account the sort of off-hand comment—someone's sotto voce remark—that sprang from ignorance, misinformation, and myth, rather than malice. We tried not to be made unhappy by bumbling insensitivity whenever we could ferret out even a tendency toward good intentions. We took care to explain as tactfully as possible that we were, in fact, the very *them* at whom their joke or remark was directed. And we're still on guard; it's a habit that's impossible to throw off.

But as I stood there holding the phone, I actually had the sensation of tension dissolving across my back and shoulders, and in the pit of my stomach, leaving me surprisingly shaky and near tears. I couldn't reply for a moment, and Sally misunderstood.

"Of course, he can certainly write a different essay, Robb. And he would never use Steve's name if you think it would intrude—"

"No, no! I think it's wonderful, Sally. I think Timothy's essay sounds great, and I don't think there's any need to check with Stephen. He's really out of the closet, Sally."

"Yes, I know." And her voice fell back into its normal tone of brisk efficiency; we had both been uneasy. "And at first I thought that it must be so hard for you and Charles, because Steve always seemed to be the perfect boy. And *then* I thought, Well, he still is! When he came out it was *brave* of him. And it was good for everybody!"

CHARLES AND I RESUMED OUR ORDINARY LIVES and, since Charles was chair of the history department, fell into an extremely harried but normal pace of work and writing all through that winter and into the summer and even right up to the evening of August 17, 1992. That night Pat Buchanan stood on the dais at the Republican National Convention, and in one short and breathtakingly nasty speech frightened us as deeply as we'd ever been frightened with his clenched-faced, sneering disparagement of gays and his characterization of the Democratic National Convention a month earlier as "the greatest single exhibition of cross-dressing in American political history." He declared that America was in a cultural and religious war for the soul of the country. He celebrated the Army's 18th Cavalry troops, M16's at the ready, reclaiming the streets of Los Angeles after the L.A. riots. He said that in the same way "we must take back our cities, and take back our culture, and take back our country." With his pretense of championing family values, Pat Buchanan placed our own family under nearly unendurable strain.

Stephen and Jack were home that summer, but they were both working long hours at summer jobs to earn enough spending money for the next school year. They were involved in their own social lives, and they weren't especially interested in the upcoming election. But Charles and I were passionately interested. We had watched the Democratic National Convention in July with growing hopefulness that the country might finally be entering an era when civil rights for gays and lesbians would be seriously addressed. For the first time in history, an openly gay man had addressed a national political convention, and the delegates had listened to him cordially and with seeming compassion. It didn't matter to us in the long run whether the Democrats' agenda was courageous or cynical; at least the existence of and discrimination against gays and lesbians had been addressed.

Within the confines of our own house, and our own town, as Charles and I occupied territory so familiar that we could navigate in any light, we had become fairly sanguine. But any ease we had reached, any optimism we had felt, was shattered by the Republican National Convention. Charles and I could hardly get through a day without being overcome with real fear, and I had trouble sleeping. It was frightening to know that there were people like Pat Buchanan out there, fomenting discord, essentially sanctioning violence in the name of promoting their agenda of old-fashioned American values.

Being constantly fearful is a terrible way to live, and it paralyzes the other senses. To perceive such danger to one of your own children raises the stakes, and Charles and I became more single-minded than we should have in our pursuit of peace of mind about Stephen's safety in the world. We got so caught up in the process of working for gay rights that we paid a hard price. In some ways we forgot about Jack, although he is as passionate an advocate for gay rights as we are. But he is working out his own life, and he had the right to expect some of our attention to be directed his way. I know from other members of

P-FLAG that this terror-wrought single-mindedness strains the internal relationships of almost every family in the same way, unwittingly directing parental attention only to the problems at hand that would affect the child most endangered.

When Jack and Stephen went back to school in September, we became even more involved in what had very nearly become a crusade as the presidential election approached. But we stayed in touch with both boys. In October, the First Congregational Church was the first church in Williamstown to declare itself an open and affirming church that would perform a Covenant of Holy Union for a gay or lesbian couple seeking to dedicate their lives to each other. We have since become members of that church, but their action was merely coincidental, having nothing to do with us, and we were elated that the church and its membership had taken such courageous action. We phoned both children immediately with that news.

In November, we were in touch with the boys off and on all day and late into the night of the election, and they phoned us during that vigil as often as we phoned them to exchange the latest rumors and updates. Jack cares passionately about political issues; in fact, he has always been a fiery advocate of civil rights and social justice for everyone. It didn't occur to us that we weren't paying attention to other issues in his life.

As the country moved into the cruel and ludicrous debate about gays in the military after the election, Charles's and my entire concentration was captured, because calls to P-FLAG increased immediately. Editorials pro and con blossomed in newspapers and magazines across the country. Letters to the editor on this subject were often little more than vicious tirades about the "gay lifestyle," whatever that is. And military men everywhere spoke out about their fear of taking *showers* with openly gay soldiers. Hysteria prevailed, and the spectacle was shameful, as hurtful and damaging as when, during the Civil Rights movement, the status of blacks as human beings was considered a matter of legitimate contention. We had several calls from gay veterans of the Vietnam War, one of whom said to me that he didn't know how he could stand to wake up one more morning and feel he had to justify his existence as a human being.

Charles and I forgot our own dictum to assume nothing, and we went about our business certain that Jack understood that our interest in his welfare and his happiness was as strong as ever, but that we simply didn't have any extra time to inquire about it. We were spending our extra time, such as it was, lobbying senators, writing letters to congressmen and columnists, responding as best we could to the daily assaults on gays and lesbians from one source or another, and therefore responding to assaults on our family.

One Sunday morning when Stephen was home from Yale in the spring of 1993, the two of us were sitting at the table reading the paper, and I glanced up to see him looking off into the distance, scowling.

"Good lord, Stephen! What's the matter with you? It's a gorgeous day outside. I thought you were going to hike to the top of Mount Greylock."

"Nothing's wrong," he said. "I was just thinking

about all the work I have to finish." And he put the paper aside and left the room.

A little later, when I cleared the table, I glanced at the paper, and there was a prominent picture of Senator Sam Nunn of Georgia, haranguing the Senate Armed Services Committee about what a disaster it would be if gays and lesbians were admitted to the military. I took the paper with me and went to find Stephen.

"Is this what you were upset about?" I asked him, when I found him on the back porch.

"It's not important, Mom. I'd rather not talk about it. I'm sick of the whole subject."

"Well, it is important, Steve. If Sam Nunn upsets you. Sam Nunn is . . . in Baton Rouge I went to school with *hundreds* of Sam Nunns. God! And some of those Sam Nunns were gay! I didn't know it *then,* but it's clear to me now. All my *uncles* were Sam Nunns, for God's sake! You just can't let people like that get to you!"

"It's easy to say that. I mean, I *do* say that, or think it. But every time I see a picture like that it makes me feel . . . wrong."

"Wrong? You mean you feel that you've done something wrong?

"No. I feel *wrong.*"

"I don't understand. I don't know how you mean. You mean that you feel it's wrong to be gay?"

"No. I mean that I feel it's wrong to *exist.* That everything about *me* is wrong. I know that's not true, but you look at Sam Nunn's face! Look at that picture! And they always describe him as 'the highly respected senator from Georgia.' So here's this guy everybody respects so much, and everything about him is like some sort of declaration that I shouldn't even exist." He forestalled my protestation. "I don't *believe* it, but I feel it, and I have to really try hard not to act on it. I have to fight hard not to pretend. Not to go back in the closet. I have to force myself to think about why I know I'm not wrong."

I've come to think of this reaction as the Sam Nunn Syndrome, because it isn't particular to Stephen; I've heard it time and again when taking P-FLAG calls. But the fury I felt that morning was very nearly incalculable. That Sam Nunn—that ghastly epitome of humorless, patriarchal, small-town, southern rectitude, who is perhaps pathologically incapable of empathy—that this arrogant, smug man could touch a child of mine and injure him, and that Sam Nunn would have been elated to know that he had done so, made me ill with rage. And the constant reminders of the Sam Nunns of the world threw me and Charles into even more fervent letter writing and telephoning.

When the summer of 1993 came around, Jack decided to get a job in Middletown and share a house with friends. This wasn't so unusual a plan for a college student his age, although I was sorry he wouldn't be at home. In fact, I had to keep myself from telling him that I really wished he would live at home for just one more summer. I didn't say anything, because I thought he would have more fun with his friends in Middletown, and I could detect some sort of strain in his voice whenever we spoke. I thought maybe it was important for him *not* to have to be around his parents all summer.

One afternoon he called me from Conneticut to tell

me a tire had blown on the car and that he was stranded at a filling station. It was a hot day, and we had guests coming for dinner. I was tired and cross when he called.

"Jack! I'm in Williamstown, and you have my car. What can I possibly do? Why don't you call AAA?"

"That's why I called. I don't have my AAA card with me, and I need you to call their 800 number and find out where the nearest—"

I was impatient. "How could you have left the house without your AAA card, Jack? I've told you a hundred times—"

"You know," he said, "I really don't think that there's any place at all for me in our family." I could hear traffic roaring by and realized that he must be phoning from an outside phone booth. His voice had suddenly gone hoarse with strain, and I was shocked.

"What? What are you talking about, Jack?"

"I'm stuck here in the middle of nowhere . . . out on the interstate. If Steve had called you for help, you wouldn't be *mad*. You'd be worried! But I almost had a wreck when the tire blew . . . you didn't even ask—"

"Oh, God, Jack! Oh, Jack . . ." I choked up and couldn't speak, but he continued.

"I know you and Dad love me. Of course I know that. And you're really good parents. I know I'm lucky to have you as parents, and I hope you know that I love you and Dad and Steve. But I just don't fit anymore. There's no room for me. Our whole family's focused on just one thing now, and I know it's important. It's important to me, too. But I feel . . . like I don't really have a home anymore."

Thank God that when Charles and I have hurt our children's feelings one way or another, they eventually let us know it. They don't just take it in stride; they give us a second chance, and we've done the same when they've hurt or saddened us. Jack has always been reluctant to complain about anything—he's a stoic—but last summer, from a phone booth at a gas station, he finally explained the reason for the distance I had known was growing between us.

"You're absolutely right, Jack," I said. "You're absolutely right, and I don't know what I can do but tell you how sorry I am—"

"But, Mom, it's nothing you've done that's *wrong*—"

"Oh, Jack, we love you more than you can possibly know, and we've just been caught up in fear and work, and we haven't been paying attention to everything we should. I wish you'd come home this weekend."

Charles and I had failed Jack in many ways that year, simply because our imagination on his behalf had shut down. We hadn't put ourselves in his shoes; we didn't know how to imagine what he might be thinking or feeling, so we just took his word for how he felt. And it wasn't that he had misrepresented himself to us; I think it's more that he thought his own problems would seem petty to us in the face of our larger concerns.

My mother once told me that when she was growing up in Nashville and just starting to be interested in boys, she had bemoaned the fact that she wasn't taller with the long legs of a movie star. Her grandmother was a stern woman, and having overheard my mother's lament turned to her and said, "You should be glad you have any legs at all! You could be in a wheelchair. You should wake up every day and be thankful that you aren't crippled!" So my mother felt even worse, having had the audacity to yearn for beautiful legs, and being instructed to be grateful for being able to walk. I don't know why my great-grandmother didn't simply tell my mother how beautiful she was, because it's something my mother has never entirely believed.

But I think that, in the same way my mother felt that she must be grateful not to be crippled, Jack had inferred that he had to be grateful not to be endangered, not to be part of a minority that has to fight for their rights at every turn. He had ceased telling us anything at all about his personal life, probably because he thought that in the grand scheme of things it would seem frivolous. Charles and I should have understood that sooner; it was a serious lapse of intuition.

Jack and I were exhausted by that brief conversation over the phone, but in the next weeks and months we went through another process of defining ourselves as a family, ordering our priorities, paying careful attention to each other. And I've noticed in my connection with P-FLAG that a good many families go through exactly the same experience, but they haven't all been as lucky as we have been. Too often siblings who were allies become estranged, and the family falls apart in their battle to cling together in the face of the tide of contempt for whichever one of them they are trying to protect. And these families, like ours, are made up of people who mean to cherish one another. But they are families—also like ours—that can lose their balance under the frenzied attacks of people like Pat Buchanan who champion family values.

JUST YESTERDAY, IN MID-JANUARY OF 1994, Charles came home from a meeting shaking his head in amusement and resignation. A friend had asked him in great detail about our experience of having a child come out, and Charles had answered every question, had explained that one must never assume anything about one's children.

His friend commented that he was sure he could assume at least one thing about his eight-year-old daughter; he was sure he could assume that she, herself, would never be prejudiced against gays, because that's how they were raising her. It hadn't crossed his mind that as his daughter's sexuality developed, she might very well wrestle with the fact that she *was* gay. He will continue on in his blithe assumptions unless or until his daughter approaches him one day and says, "Daddy, there's something I've been wanting to tell you."

Recently I had a call on the P-FLAG helpline from a student at the college who has been having a terrible time with his parents since early fall, when he had worked up his courage to tell them he was gay.

"Well," I said, "what has your relationship been like with your parents up until this point?"

"Great," he said. "Really great. Maybe that's one of the reasons I feel so bad. I never expected them to be so . . . I don't know . . . it's like they feel I've betrayed them. My mother just cries and cries. She won't talk to me . . . ," and his voice broke, so I talked a little while to give him a chance to regain his poise, because he was clearly embarrassed. He hadn't told me anything about himself; I didn't even know his name, so I began running through a litany of possibilities.

"You know, maybe your parents are just deeply shaken because of long held religious beliefs, or maybe living in a conservative area of the country, or whatever ethnic background they come from, can sometimes make it difficult—"

"My parents marched in the gay rights parade with my mother's brother. My mother's *brother* is gay!"

I was at a loss, and before I thought better of it I wondered out loud to him, "Well, then, what on earth could be the problem?"

"I don't know. I don't know. I've done everything I could to make them proud of me. I was third in my class in high school. I was student council president, a class speaker. I was a first-string linebacker on the football team, and we went to the state championships. I'm on full financial aid here. . . . But my mother says she can't stand it. She doesn't ever want to hear about me being gay. She says that it's one thing to be for gay rights, but that it's different when it's your own child."

I shut my eyes, as if that would close out the description of his mother's reaction to him. I knew what had happened; his mother couldn't bear the idea of her own son being gay, because he had so much to lose. But I've heard similar stories from teenagers who are not so accomplished, who have already failed to meet their parents' expectations scholastically or socially, and therefore their parents perceive the news of that child's homosexuality as the last straw, as the end of hope on their own child's behalf.

"It's going to be fine," I said. "Your parents are going to be just fine about this, but it's going to take them a little while." I know it's unwise to say anything so absolute, but I am certain that this student and his parents—with good luck—will get through this patch of confusion and reassessment.

"But I don't think my mother's ever going to have a conversation with me again. I walk in the door and she's out of there. If we're together for over two minutes, she starts to cry. She told me . . . she told me it would have been easier for her if I had *died*."

"She doesn't mean that! She really doesn't mean that!" I know that if anything happens to this boy, his mother will be guilt ridden for the rest of her life. Parents don't have the luxury of making mistakes of this magnitude, although most of the parents I know—of children straight or gay—have at one time or another said something to their children that they know is unforgivable. Most of their children, however, are not as vulnerable as the young man I was talking to on the phone.

"You've got to give her a little time," I said, but he was silent on the other end of the line, and when he spoke I could hear that he was holding back tears.

"I don't think I can talk about this," he said, and hung up. Every day I check the paper to be sure that no Williams student has come to harm, because I don't know who this young man is, and even if I did, there is very little I could do to help him except to offer him reassurance.

But I think of him all the time. When I am on the grounds of the college, I find myself searching the faces of the young men I pass by, as if I could spot that sad and desperate boy who is no doubt practiced and adept at concealment. I think of him every day. I wake up in the early hours of the morning worrying about him. In a way, he has become every child lost to despair, to self-loathing, to the pettiness and stupidity of the world around him. He has become in my imagination every child who believes he or she alone is responsible for maintaining family happiness.

CHILDREN SHOULDN'T BE BURDENED with the responsibility for their parents' happiness. And parents don't have the right to appropriate either the successes or the failures in the lives of their children. But it takes parents—including me and Charles—longer than it should to understand that. This book is by way of giving their lives back to my own sons, of liberating them from being responsible for our happiness, and of indicating to them that we do love them absolutely and unconditionally.

But this memoir is not about Stephen and Jack. I only *know* them as my children, and they are trapped here in these pages by my idea of them when they were only seventeen and nineteen. This book isn't even about Stephen's coming out as a gay man. I don't know when he came out to anyone else; I don't know the pain he must have suffered trying to conceal an essential part of himself. I don't know who was the first person he told or the fear he might have felt at first making that declaration. And I don't know if it was difficult for Jack to come to terms with this new definition of his brother, of his whole family.

My children have behaved with grace and courage in letting me tell this story. I am especially concerned that I not co-opt their own histories and hinder them in any attempt they might eventually make to discover and re-define their pasts, to tell their own stories. It is, I believe, a mark of the generosity of everyone in my family that they have encouraged me to continue with this book as they have read it chapter by chapter, even though the reconstruction of a time of such distress and bafflement has often been painful for all of us. This book is, in part, about making amends to my children for our occasional clumsiness as parents, and, since writing is the only way I've hit upon to be conversant with the world, it seems to me, in retrospect, that writing this book was the least that I could do.

Author's Note

I AM NOT USING THE REAL NAMES of anyone, other than my immediate family, who isn't already a public person, because privacy is valuable, and also because memory is subjective. I have to leave the past for each person to interpret for him or herself.

ANYONE INTERESTED IN CONTACTING the non-profit organization, P-FLAG (Parents, Families, and Friends of Lesbians and Gays Inc.) may write to: P-FLAG, 1012 14th St. NW, Washington, DC 20005 (202-638-4200).